Down in the Deep

Written by
Anne Cotton
and
Fran Martin

Illustrated by Lyn Hope

Published by
Teaching Resource Center
P.O. Box 1509
San Leandro, CA 94577

Printed in the United States of America
ISBN: 1–56785–014–6

Contents

The Basic Teaching Strategies

In the development of this theme you will find phrases as **brainstorm for, develop in the pocket chart, sort and classify,** etc. To help clarify these phrases we have listed these basic teaching strategies and have given a brief description of each.

Fill with language:

This is when we read to the children. We read not only stories but poetry and factual information as well. We begin with a discussion of the illustrations to develop as much oral language as possible. We stop periodically to provide the opportunity for the child to anticipate and predict what might happen next. We also read a selection many times over to help make that selection become a part of the child. We feel strongly that we must continually *fill the child with language* as we move ahead with the theme.

Chanting:

Children need to work orally with the patterns of language. The primary way to do this with very young children is by chanting. This technique helps instill the rhythm and structure of language which then becomes a part of their everyday speech.

One way to chant is by using the my turn, your turn technique. The teacher reads a phrase and the children echo this phrase. The teacher tracks (runs hand under the text, pointing to each word) as the chanting takes place. Children may chant using the whole text (pictures, pictures and words, or words alone), or merely chant a repetitive phrase ("Not I," said the dog.[2]) Chanting may be done using big books, charts, brainstorming ideas, pocket chart activities, trade books, etc. Songs and poems should also be included. When working with songs and poetry, we often add rhythmic hand movements which help instill the rhythm of the language and enhances the memorization.

Brainstorming:

Brainstorming is when children orally respond to a question posed by the teacher with the results usually being recorded where they may be seen by the children. This gives the teacher an insight into the children's knowledge. We usually begin a theme by brainstorming for what the children know about a given subject. A lack of ideas indicates that the children may need a *refill* of language and knowledge. The brainstorming is continuously being added to as the theme is developed.

Brainstorming is a whole class activity. The teacher begins by asking a question such as "What is green?" and elicits responses from the children. As the children respond, the teacher draws the appropriate pictures on the chalkboard and the children chant. **Note:** at the beginning of the kindergarten year, draw a picture only. No words are needed.

After the brainstorming, again chant all the pictures that were drawn: "A leaf is green. A turtle is green. Grass is green. A car is green." As the year progresses you will want to add words to the brainstorming:

Most brainstorming needs to be saved! As you work through a theme you will be continually referring to these ideas. Copy the brainstorming onto cards or chart paper. The cards may be displayed using masking tape, sticky side out. (See picture on page 6.) The chart may be used for matching and rebuilding. At a later date the chart may be cut apart and made into a strip book.

Another example of a brainstorming technique is to record ideas in categories that are not labeled. After the pattern is obvious, the children tell where to record the next idea. This method helps stimulate the children's thinking.

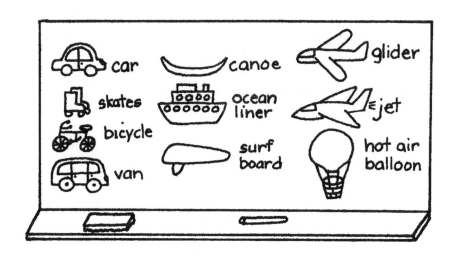

Sorting and Classifying:

This when children look for likenesses and differences and put things together that are alike in some manner. The ideas from brainstorming activities are ideal for sorting and classifying. We usually begin classifying with groups of four to six children, with each group having about twenty cards or items to sort.

After this small group sorting activity, the whole class regroups and chants. Example: We classified according to color and then chanted, "A chair is green. An olive is green. A fat frog is green, etc." Gradually, we work toward activities that will involve individual classifications. The results of these activities may be graphed, producing either a real graph or a pictorial graph.[3]

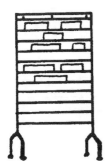

Develop in the Pocket Chart:

We use a pocket chart made of clear acetate and nylon.[4] You may use sentence strips or tagboard cards (laminated or contacted for a longer life) with the pocket chart. Whole texts, repeated phrases or pictures only may be used. There are a variety of ways to use the pocket chart. We listed our favorites:

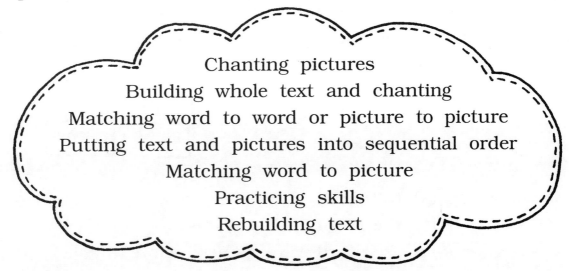

Chanting pictures
Building whole text and chanting
Matching word to word or picture to picture
Putting text and pictures into sequential order
Matching word to picture
Practicing skills
Rebuilding text

When we are developing a lesson in the pocket chart, we usually insert the appropriate pictures, or text and pictures, and then have the children chant **many** times. We may ask the children to hide their eyes and then we take something out of the text or merely turn it over.

The children then decide what is missing and chant to see if they are correct. We then take more than one word, picture, or phrase out (or turn them over) and repeat the process. The final task is to rebuild the entire text.

Samples:

Step 1:   Chanting pictures
             "A leaf is green."

Step 2:	Build whole text and chant: "A leaf is green."	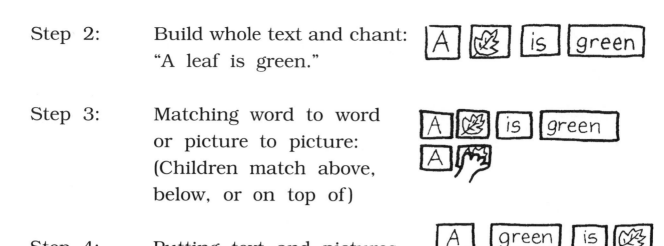

Step 3:	Matching word to word or picture to picture: (Children match above, below, or on top of)

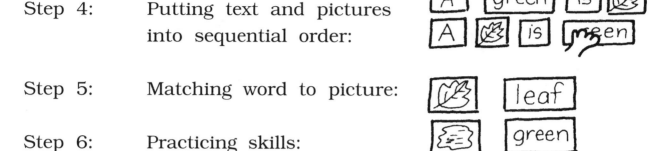

Step 4:	Putting text and pictures into sequential order:

Step 5:	Matching word to picture:
Step 6:	Practicing skills:

- Find the word that says *green*.
- Find the word that says *is*.
- Find the word that comes before *green*.
- Find the word that comes after *is*.
- What sound do you hear at the beginning of the word *leaf*?

Step 7:   Rebuilding: All pictures and text are distributed to the children and the complete story is built again in the pocket chart. Children read the text from the pocket chart, checking for accuracy.

Tracking:

This involves moving your hand under and pointing to each word as it is read. This helps develop left to right progression as well as one-to-one correspondence between the printed text and the spoken word.

Big Books:

These are enlarged versions of books, poems or songs. The print must be large enough so that it may be seen by the entire class. The enlarged print allows us to track as we read and helps to develop one-to-one correspondence. Many of the activities used with the pocket chart may also be used with big books. We laminate the pages of teacher-prepared big books and bind them with loose leaf rings. The rings may be taken out and the pages shuffled so that the children may sequence the big book. For obvious reasons **do not** number the pages. These books are really loved and used over and over by the children.

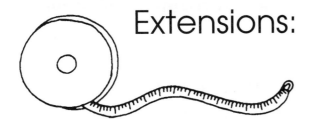

Extensions:

These are activities we practice what we learned during brain-storming, reading, chanting, and the various pocket chart activities. We try to incorporate the following:

Individual booklets – Each child makes his/her own booklet and should have the opportunity to read and track before taking it home.

Class book – Each child contributes a page and the book is kept in the classroom library.

Drama – Children act out the activity with **all** children taking **all** the parts. (a bit noisy but very effective)

Art – Children make illustrations for bulletin boards, booklets, plays, etc., using as many different kinds of art media as possible.

Make-a-play – Children retell a story by manipulating characters they have made.

Writing – All writing activities need to be extensively developed orally **first.**

1. Using a structure or frame, the children fill in the blanks by taking the ideas from the brainstorming activities.

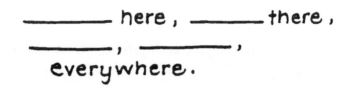

2. Creating innovations: children orally rewrite a familiar text using their own words. Example: (change "Brown bear, brown bear, what do you see?" to "Octopus, Octopus, what do you see?") This can be an individual or a whole group activity. The teacher may need to take dictation for the very young child.

3. Dictation: children individually illustrate and the teacher transcribes for them.

Draw with me – This is a whole class activity where language development is the goal. We do not consider this an art lesson. All the children are working with individual chalkboards at this time. We ask the children to name all the parts that need to be included to draw a specific object. A sample might be:

"What do we need to make a house?"

"A door"

"A roof"

"Windows"

(continue until entire picture is completed)

Individual sequencing – This is when each child puts pictures or a text into a specific order. This is usually a *cut and paste* activity. It varies in difficulty. We begin with pictures only, then pictures with the text, and finally the text alone. We also put the text in sequence with numerals, words, and pictures.

Pictures only:

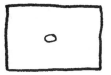 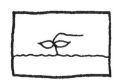  

Pictures with text:

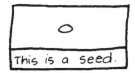   

Numeral, text and picture:

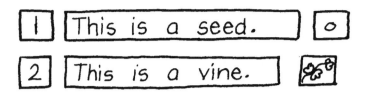

Homework – This is when we try to involve the family. The homework is occasional and we include a detailed explanation. This activity is returned to class and used for chanting, classifying booklet making or other language activities.

An example might be:

Dear Parents,

Our language arts theme this month is centered around plants. This week we are learning about seeds. Your child needs to bring a picture of something that grows from a seed. You may help your child draw or find a picture in a magazine. Please return the picture tomorrow.

Thank you for helping!

A follow-up activity might include sorting and classifying these pictures according to whether the plant produces food or not, i.e., flower, grapes, oak tree, oranges, etc. A booklet can then be made including all the homework pictures or individual booklets may be made from each classification.

---

1. Martin, Jr., Bill. *Brown Bear,* Holt, Rinehart and Winston, New York, NY, 1970.
2. Galdone, Paul. *Little Red Hen,* Clarion Books, New York, NY, 1973.
3. Baratta-Lorton, Mary. *Mathematics Their Way,* Addison-Wesley Publishing Company, Reading, MA, 1976.
4. Available through **Teaching Resource Center**, P.O. Box 1509, 14023 Catalina Street, San Leandro, CA 94577.

Introduction

Before you begin this theme, you will want to create an environment that will stimulate interest in the sea. We like to hang a fish net looped over a wire that stretches the length of the classroom. Attach cork and colorful cutouts of fish (you will replace these cutouts with artwork from the children as the theme progresses). Intersperse long crepe paper streamers in blues and greens to create a *down in the deep* atmosphere.

It is nice to have large posters of whales, sharks, etc. and a display of sea shells. You will also want to have a collection of informational books about sea life and add to this collection as the theme is developed.

If you wish to use the big books offered through The Big Book Bin (*I Took A Trip Down To The Sea; One, One, the Beach Is Fun* and *Octopus*) we suggest you send for them 3–4 weeks before you want to begin this theme as it takes a while for the books to arrive and you will need time to prepare them. The address is *The Big Book Bin Inc., P.O. Box 800-480, Abbotsford, B.C. V2S 6H1, Canada.*

A resource that we like is the Sea Animals theme written by Pat Perea. It is part of her *Come With Me Science Series.* This science resource deals with lobsters, squids, seahorses, starfish and hermit crabs. Also available is a brand new Ocean Ecosystem (both Atlantic and Pacific). If you are interested, the address is S/S Publishing Co., 3550 Durock Road, Shingle Springs, CA. 95682. Phone: 1-916-677-1545.

It is not our intent to dwell extensively on any one aspect of sea life – rather, this theme is meant to be very general in nature. It would be fun to develop a complete theme on any one of the sea creatures (whales, fish, crabs, etc.) and **Down In The Deep** would be a great introduction. It is conceivable to do a sea life theme the entire year! The ideas are endless!

Although we write our themes in a specific sequence they are merely suggestions. You need not follow this exact order. Choose those activities that best suit your classroom. **Down In The Deep** is a favorite with children and we hope it will be one of yours, too.

At the time this book went to press, all the books we have developed were in print. However, books are going in and out of print all the time. If you cannot locate a particular book, try the public library, your school library or contact a local bookstore and they might be able to track the selection down for you. Happy fishing!

Theme At A Glance

Trade Books & Big Books

A House For Hermit Crab
Big Al
Down By The Bay
Fish Eyes
Five Silly Fishermen
Four Brave Sailors
Herman The Helper
Is This A House For Hermit Crab?
Mr. Gumpy's Outing
The Twelve Days Of Summer
What's In The Deep Blue Sea?
Who Sank The Boat?

Down In The Deep
I Took A Trip Down To
     The Sea
Octopus
One, One, The Beach Is
     Fun

Class Books & Booklets

An Octopus Can
Down In The Deep
I Took A Trip Down To The Sea
One, One, A Day In The Sun
Our Outings
Twelve Days Of Summer

Down By The Blue Sea
Fishy Facts
Hole In The Bottom Of The
     Sea

Songs

Down By The Bay
Down In The Deep
I Took A Trip Down To The Sea
Long-legged Sailor
Octopus
Oyster In The Deep
There's A Hole In The Bottom Of The Sea

Art

Sea Silhouettes
Herman The Helper Octopus
Stuffed Sea Creatures
Shape Fish & Tissue Seaweed
Hermit Crab Art
Paper Plate Fish & Oyster
Mural of Fish With The Deep Sea Smile
Ocean Habitat
Twelve Days Of Summer

Science & Math

Sea Animal Sorting
Sink or Float
Oyster "Fact" Book
Come With Me Science - Sea Animals
Sorting Sea Creatures By Ocean Habitat

Fishy Facts - addition equations

Whale Game - Math Their Way

Drama
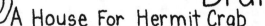
A House For Hermit Crab
Fish
Five Little Fishies
Five Silly Fishermen - Make-A-Play
I Took A Trip Down To The Sea
Mr. Gumpy's Outing
What's In The Deep Blue Sea?

Activity 1 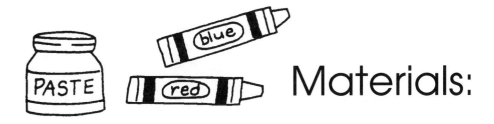 _Big Al_

Materials:

Materials needed:

- _Big Al_ by Andrew Clements
- Sea creatures, blacklines 1–5 for a noun wordbank
- Blackline 6 of the scary fish
- Blue butcher paper for bulletin board
- Tan butcher paper for bulletin board
- Sentence strips
- Felt pens
- Large easel paper
- Tempra paints
- Fat string
- Three fish hooks (bent paper clips will do) for the bulletin board
- Black construction paper for the bulletin board fishing poles

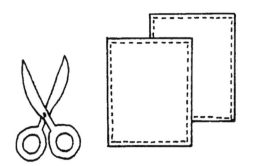

Preparation:

1. Cut fifteen sentence strips in half to use with the sea creature pictures we have provided.
2. Color and cut blacklines 1–5 for the noun wordbank. **Note:** You may want to add any other small pictures of sea creatures that you have available.
3. Glue each picture from blacklines 1–5 to the left side of the pre-cut sentence strips. Print the appropriate word with felt pen. Laminate or contact.

4. If you live near the shore or a large aquarium it is possible to purchase preserved varieties of fish and you may wish to select your own scary fish. (A porcupine fish works really well.) If you are not fortunate enough to live by the water you may wish to color, mount and laminate blackline 6 of the scary fish.
5. To prepare the bulletin board, cut blue butcher paper for the water and tan for the sandy bottom. Add a boat. To make fishing poles, roll black construction paper into about a quarter inch diameter tube and attach string and hook. (See picture of completed bulletin board under Extension.)

6. Print the following on sentence strips and save these for the bulletin board:

blue green eyes and whiskers three
electric lights up and down his tail
terrible teeth
long, strong jaws
long stalked eyes
terrible claws
laughing eye
deep sea smile

Procedure:

1. Begin this lesson by presenting a sample or picture of a scary fish. Discuss the attributes of the fish and draw from the children words that describe it. Continue until the children have established that this fish is definitely unattractive.

2. Tell the children you have a story about a fish that was really fierce looking and his name was Big Al. Read and enjoy this delightful story by Andrew Clements. This book provides an opportunity to discuss the real qualities of friendship and promotes the idea that appearances have nothing to do with these qualities.

3. Create a noun wordbank by brainstorming on the chalkboard for other animals that live in the sea. Chant each of the ideas as they are listed – "A shark lives down in the deep. A whale lives down in the deep."

4. A permanent wordbank may be made by using the thirty-six pictures of sea animals that we have provided. You will want to only use those that your children think of and add to the wordbank as the theme progresses and as the children gain more knowledge. Other sources of pictures are color books, *National Geographic,* and other children's nature magazines.

5. Tell the children you are going to read a poem about some really different looking fish. Read the poem *The Fish With The Deep Sea Smile* by Margaret Wise Brown.

The Fish With The Deep Sea Smile

They fished and they fished
Way down in the sea
Down in the sea a mile
They fished among all the fish in the sea
For the fish with the deep sea smile.

One fish came up from the deep of the sea
From down in the sea a mile
It had blue green eyes
And whiskers three
But never a deep sea smile.

One fish came up from the deep of the sea
From down in the sea a mile
With electric lights up and down his tail
But never a deep sea smile.

They fished and they fished
Way down in the sea
Down in the sea a mile
They fished among all the fish in the sea
For the fish with the deep sea smile.

One fish came up with terrible teeth
One fish with long strong jaws
One fish came up with long stalked eyes
One fish with terrible claws.

They fished all through the ocean deep
For many and many a mile
And they caught a fish with a laughing eye
But none with a deep sea smile.

And then one day they got a pull
From down in the sea a mile
And when they pulled the fish into the boat
HE SMILED A DEEP SEA SMILE.

And as he smiled, the hook got free
And then, what a deep sea smile!
He flipped his tail and swam away
Down in the sea a mile.

6. Ask the children how the *fish with the deep sea smile* got away. Have the children smile for their neighbor and then discuss what they do with their mouths when they smile. Develop the meaning of such words as: stalked eye, laughing eye, terrible teeth, strong jaws, electric lights, terrible claws and deep sea smile.

7. Before re-reading the poem, tell the children you will ask them to describe the different fish that were in the poem and to listen carefully to the describing words. Re-read the poem.

8. Using the chalkboard, help the children list all the different fish as they are mentioned. Be sure not to illustrate as the children will be doing this during the extension activity.

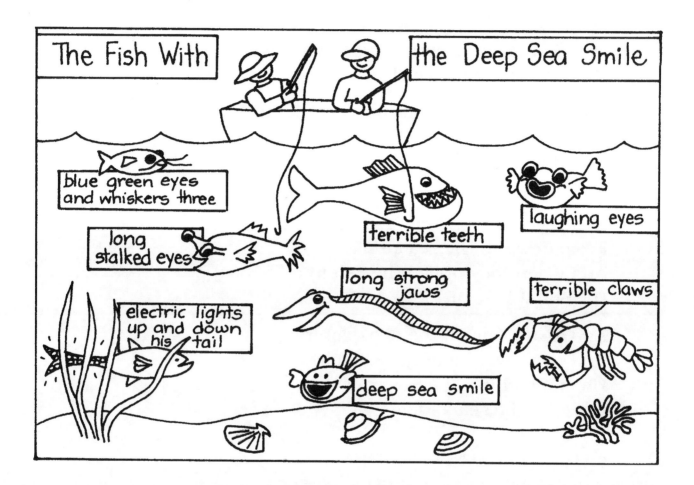

You will want to make sure each child is able to contribute to this mural. Items you might want to include are:

- fishermen
- fish with blue green eyes and whiskers three
- fish with electric lights up and down his tail
- fish with terrible teeth

- fish with long strong jaws
- fish with long stalked eyes
- fish with terrible claws
- fish with a laughing eye
- fish with a deep sea smile
- seaweed
- shells
- coral
- starfish
- rocks
- clouds
- sun

We suggest the children paint the items on large easel paper. When they are dry, outline with a broad black felt pen or with black tempra and then cut them out.

Arrange the paintings on the bulletin board and add the sentence strip labels. After the bulletin board is up, read the poem again and admire the artwork! You will find that the children will read this bulletin board over and over.

Activity 2

I Took A Trip Down To The Sea

Materials:

Materials needed:

- *I Took A Trip Down To The Sea*, big book available through The Big Book Bin (see introduction)
- Blacklines 7–8 for pocket chart pictures
- Blackline nine for kindergarten class book
- Sentence strips
- Felt pens
- Laminating film or contact paper
- Factual books about sea life
- Set of animal picture cards, including sea animals
- 10 pieces of 4″ x 5″ tagboard cards for the pocket chart.

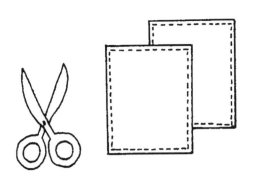

Preparation:

1. Color, cut and mount the pictures from blacklines 7–8 on 4" x 5" tagboard cards. Contact or laminate.
2. Color and laminate the big book, *I Took A Trip Down To The Sea*
3. On sentence strips print the following:

I took a trip down to the sea.

What do you s'pose I saw?

I saw

and it

La, la, la, la, la, la.

4. Using the big book as a guide, print on sentence strips the sea animal names and what the animals are doing.

a whale

spouted at me

5. Copy the last two lines of the big book on sentence strips.
6. For kindergarten, duplicate blackline 9, one per child, for a class book.

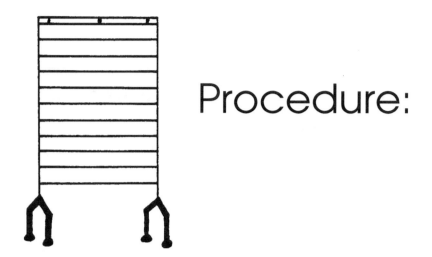

Procedure:

Note: The big book, *I Took A Trip Down To The Sea,* can be sung, using the same melody as *I Took A Trip To Grandfathers Farm.* This song is found on the Hap Palmer record, *Witches Brew.*

1. To add to the children's knowledge about sea life, tell the class that you are going to read a special book that describes life in the sea. Ask them to listen carefully, because when you are through, you are going to ask them to list more animals for the wordbank. (This was begun in Activity 1)
2. Read a factual book about the sea. Two that we like to use are *Discover Ocean Life* by Alice Jablonsky and *Water Life* by Ken Hoy. After reading, help the children add to the noun wordbank. Chant or read each animal.
3. Introduce the big book, *I Took A Trip Down To The Sea.* Sing and enjoy. Add any new animals to the wordbank. Sing again and

develop the vocabulary, verse by verse, by dramatizing the verbs. (spouted, scuttled, squirted, stared, peered, skimmed, clung) Sing the song again, using the my turn, your turn technique.

4. Ask the children to try to name all the different animals that were in the song. Place the animal pictures in the pocket chart as they are mentioned. (**Note:** We are not convinced that it is necessary to sequence these pictures – in fact, it is difficult to remember the actual order!) Sing the song again, using the big book, to check for accuracy. Add any animals that were omitted.

5. Display the names of the animals (that you printed on sentence strips) in a second pocket chart or in a place that they will be easily accessible to the children. Using phonetic clues, help the children match the animal name to the corresponding picture. Read (a whale, a squid, etc.).

6. Guide the children in matching the action phrases (spouted at me) to the correct picture. Because these are difficult words to remember you may wish to use both phonetic clues and dramatization to help the children. Read from the pocket chart. (a whale – spouted at me, a shark – skimmed past me, etc.)

7. For first grade, play *Charades.* After the children are familiar with the action phrases, place those cards face down in a pile. Ask two or three children to come up and draw the first card. Caution them to take care and not let the class see what they have drawn. Give the children a few minutes to move away from the group and plan the dramatization that they will use. These children act out the action phrase and call on classmates to try to figure out the animal and what it is doing.

8. Place in the pocket chart the structure that was prepared in step 3 under Preparation. Place the pictures and word cards in a second pocket chart so they are accessible to the children. Build and sing each verse of the song.

9. Another way to enjoy this book and song is to divide the class in half and have one half sing the question and the second half sing the answer.

Extension: *Class book and Sorting and Classification*

1. **Sorting and Classifying** – Using a set of animal cards, help the children sort and classify by whether or not the animal is a sea creature. Divide your class into groups of 4–6 and give each group about twenty animal cards. Ask them to make three piles: animals that live in the sea, animals that don't live in the sea and a third pile for *I don't know.*

Each group brings all three stacks and places them by the pocket chart. At this point, discuss the animals that are in the *I don't know* pile. The class works together to decide into which pile to put the animals. If no one knows, offer that animal to a child for research, either at home or in the school library.

Place all the cards of animals that live in the sea in the pocket chart. Chant:

"A _____ lives in the sea." "A _____ is a sea creature."
"You can see _____ in the ocean." etc.

2. **Class Book** – Referring to the noun wordbank, the children pick several animals (not in the original song) and brainstorm for action phrases appropriate for those animals. (an octopus – waved at me, a flying fish – soared over me, a sea horse floated by me, etc.) List these on the chalkboard and chant as each new animal is added, i.e., "I saw an octopus and it waved at me." Brainstorm until you have at least twenty different animals as you want to have a variety in your book. Some of the action phrases might be appropriate for more than one animal so the children are able to mix and match some of the ideas.

2. **Kindergarten** – Each child needs one copy of blackline 9. Using the brainstorming on the chalkboard, along with the noun wordbank, the children choose one animal and one action phrase. Depending on the time of the year, you may wish to take dictation or have the children copy from the board. The children then illustrate. Bind these pages together into a book. Make a cover of your choice, read and add to your class library.

3. **First Grade** – You will make the same class book except the children will do all of the writing themselves.

Activity 3

Down in the Deep

Materials:

Materials needed:

- *Down By The Bay* by Raffi and Nadine Bernard Westcott
- Backlines 10–24 for making the big book
- Sentence strips
- Felt pens
- Pictures from the noun wordbank
- 12″ x 18″ dark blue construction paper for making the big book
- Blackline 25 for class book
- 12″ x 18″ white construction paper for the art project
- Colored chalk – sea colors
- Black construction paper for sea silhouettes
- Loose leaf rings

Preparation:

1. For the big book, color and cut blacklines 10–24. Print the text with felt pens on sentence strips. Text is as follows:

> **Down in the deep,**
> **where the seaweed grows,**
> **Back to my home**
> **I dare not go**
> **For if I do**
> **my mother will say,**
> **"Did you ever see...**
> **a clam – playing with a lamb**
> **a whale – carrying a pail**
> **a seal – fixing a meal**
> **a squid – with a little kid**
> **a fish – washing a dish**
> **an eel – making a deal**
> **a dolphin – doing some golfing**
> **a shark – trying to bark**
> **a lobster – dressed like a mobster**
> **a shrimp – with a limp**

2. Glue each picture and the corresponding sentence strips on dark blue 12″ x 18″ construction paper. Note that each verse is prepared in the same manner as the page "a clam – playing with a lamb."

3. Laminate or contact and bind with loose leaf rings.

cover

Down in the deep

Where the seaweed grows

page 1 (chorus)

Back to my home

page 2 (chorus)

I dare not go

For if I do

page 3 (chorus)

My mother will say

Did you ever see...

page 4 (chorus)

a clam

playing with a lamb

page 5 (verse 1)

4. The melody for this song may be found in *Down By The Bay*, published by Crown Publishers, Inc. or on the Raffi record or tape *Singable Songs for the Very Young.*

Our big book will be sung or read in the following manner:

> Down in the deep, where the seaweed grows,
> Back to my home, I dare not go.
> For if I do my mother will say,
> "Did you ever see a clam playing with a lamb
> Down in the deep?"

> Down in the deep, where the seaweed grows,
> Back to my home, I dare not go.
> For if I do my mother will say,
> "Did you ever see a whale carrying a pail
> Down in the deep?"
> etc.

Please note:
A. The first four pages of this big book will be sung at the beginning of each verse, followed by a rhyming couplet page.
B. The cover of this big book is to be used after each of the ten rhyming couplets. This will complete each verse with, "Down in the deep."
C. The remaining pages are the rhyming couplets for each verse.

Our philosophy concerning big books is that we feel the print needs to be large enough so that your entire class is able to see and follow along. Following this philosophy we attempted to insert the first four pages before each rhyming couplet and ended up with the world's largest big book – too cumbersome! We then tried to print all the words of the first four pages on a single page (to be inserted before each rhyming couplet) and found that the print would be too small. So, back to square one – we like the words in big print and don't think it is too difficult for you to return to the cover after each verse.

5. Duplicate blackline 25, one per child, for the class book.

Procedure:

1. If you did not do Activities 1 or 2, you will need to have your class brainstorm for a noun wordbank of sea creatures. Chant, or read, using your own frame or one of the following:

   _____ lives down in the deep.

   _____ is a sea creature.

   _____ can swim in the sea.

2. Tell the children that you have a silly song about some of the creatures that they thought of in the noun wordbank. Using the big book, introduce the song, *Down In the Deep.*

3. Sing the song again, using the my turn, your turn technique. Another way to sing this song is to divide the class into two groups. One group will sing the first four pages, the second group will sing the mother's reply, beginning with "Did you ever see..." and both groups will sing the final phrase "Down in the deep."

4. Sing Raffi's book, *Down by the Bay.* Compare and contrast the two versions of this song.

5. Have the children recall the rhyming words that are found in this song. Referring to the **noun** wordbank the children will now create a **rhyming** wordbank. (This will be used to create rhyming couplets for the class book.) Ask the children to name their favorite sea creatures and list them on the chalkboard. Help the class list words that rhyme with each particular animal that is chosen.

```
Rhyming    Wordbank
squid- lid           eel- meal           whale-jail
       kid                seal                 pail
       grid               deal                 tail
       Sid                heel                 sail
                          keel                 mail
shark- bark               wheel                nail
       park               peel
       stark              kneel          fish- wish
       lark                                    dish
       dark                                    swish
                                               Trish
```

6. Orally help the children create many rhyming couplets, referring to the rhyming wordbank for ideas. You may need to help children with the meter by clapping the rhythm to assist them with either adding or deleting words or syllables.

7. Distribute copies of blackline 25 to the class. Each child chooses one sea creature and creates a rhyming couplet. We suggest each child tell you the couplet he or she has created so you can assist if need be. (First grade children should be able to write the words while you may need to take dictation for kindergarten children.)

8. After the writing is completed, each child illustrates the couplet and these are collected. Create a cover and bind into a class book. Read and add to your class library.

Extension: *Sea Creature Silhouettes*

1. Distribute 12″ x 18″ white construction paper, one per child, and colored chalk to the class.

2. Using a sponge, wet the white construction paper. The children create an ocean by using the side of the chalk and coloring from one edge to the other. (Encourage the children to blend the sea colors.)

3. While the chalk ocean is drying, distribute black construction paper to the class. The children use white chalk and draw sea creatures, seaweed, etc. and then cut them out. Using the cut out silhouettes, the children arrange a seascape and glue these down, being careful to put the glue on the side with the chalk lines.

4. You might want to have the children create a short story about their pictures and create a class book or arrange the art and stories on a bulletin board.

Activity 4 — *Charlie Over The Ocean*

Materials:

Materials Needed:

- Sentence strips
- Felt pens
- Blacklines 26–27 for the pocket chart *and* booklet
- Blacklines 28–32 for the cover and words to the booklet
- Sandpaper
- Dark and light blue construction paper for the booklet
- Pictures from noun wordbank (used in Activities 1–3)
- Globe
- 8 pieces of 5″ x 6″ tagboard cards for the pocket chart

Preparation:

1. On sentence strips print the following:

> **Charlie over the ocean,**
> **Charlie over the sea,**
> **Charlie caught a big fish**
> **But he can't catch me!**

2. Cut these sentence strips apart into individual word cards **except** for *a big fish* – leave these three words on one card.

   You will need several blank sentence strips that will be used for any additional ideas that may arise during the rewriting of this poem. Also, you may wish to print the names of the children in your class as you will substitute the children's names for *Charlie*. However, each name needs to be written three times. After printing this 90+ times, we tend to talk to ourselves, so we do this part of the lesson orally. We will leave this up to you!

Down By The Blue Sea: Pocket Chart
3. Print the following on sentence strips. Cut into individual word cards, except for the three words *A little fish* – leave these on one card.

> **Down by the blue sea,**
> **What can it be?**
> **A little fish, a little fish,**
> **That's what I see.**

Cut the following in the same manner as you did *A little fish.*

> A big whale, a big whale,
> A starfish, a starfish,
> A seahorse, a seahorse,
> A black seal, a black seal,
> A seashell, a seashell,
> A sailboat, a sailboat,
> A sandy beach, a sandy beach,
> Me in a bathing suit,

4. **Important:** You will be using blacklines 26 and 27 for both the pocket chart and the children's individual booklets. It is necessary for you to make additional blacklines of 26 and 27 in order to have it available for future use. For the pocket chart pictures you will also need to cut a piece of brown construction paper the same size as the pocket chart pictures to represent the sandy beach.
5. Color, cut and mount the original blacklines 26–27 on 5″ x 6″ tagboard cards. Add the brown construction paper sandy beach, after implementing step 4. (These are pocket chart pictures.) Contact or laminate.

Down By The Blue Sea: **Booklet**
6. Duplicate your new blacklines 26–27, one per child, on white construction paper. You may wish to cut these apart and save for the appropriate time.
7. For kindergarten, duplicate blacklines 28–32 of the cover and words for the booklet, one page per child. Cut in half.
   Note: For first grade you may wish to have your children write the words. We give the children 8″ x 4½″ lined writing paper and have the children copy the words from the pocket chart or from the chalkboard. If your children do write the words, you will need to alter the cover blackline. Make two copies of blackline 28, cut

and paste two copies of the cover to make a new blackline master.

8. Cut sandpaper strips 1½" x 9", two per child.

9. For the front and back booklet cover, each child will need two pieces of 9" x 6" dark blue construction paper.

10. For the individual pages, each child will need nine pieces of 9" x 6" light blue construction paper.

11. For the ocean part of each page, each child will need nine pieces of 9" x 3" dark blue construction paper.

Note: You will need to prepare your own copy of *Down By The Blue Sea* before presenting the lesson to the children. The directions are found under the Extension for this activity.

12. Print the following on sentence strips and cut into individual word cards:

> **Ocean, Ocean**
> **Deep and blue.**
> **Ocean, Ocean,**
> **Old, not new.**
>
> **Ocean, Ocean,**
> **Oh, so wide.**
> **Ocean, Ocean,**
> **Big ships ride.**

13. Print the following, four times each, on sentence strips and cut into individual word cards: **Pacific, Atlantic, Indian, Arctic.**

Procedure:

1. Introduce this lesson by placing the words to *Charlie Over The Ocean* in the pocket chart and chant or read. Repeat several times, tracking as you progress. Continue until the children have committed the poem to memory.

2. Take all the word cards out of the pocket chart and distribute them to the children. Help the children rebuild this poem, word by word, and chant or read to check for accuracy.

3. Display the noun wordbank (that was developed in Activity 1 and 2) so that the individual cards are easily accessible to the children.

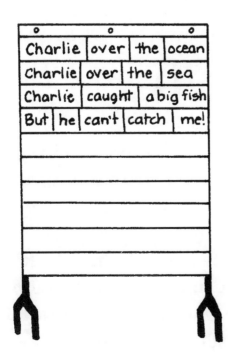

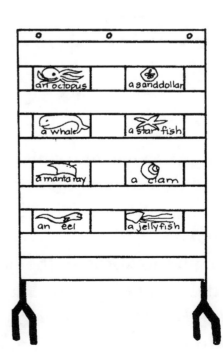

4. Remove the word card printed with *a big fish.* Using the word-bank as a guide, the children choose other sea creatures that Charlie could catch. Insert each one in the pocket chart and read or chant the new version. If the children think of an animal that is not in your noun wordbank, print that word on one of the blank sentence strips and insert that in the pocket chart.

5. If you have decided to print the class names on word cards, now is the time to use them. Choose a child and ask, "What would you like to catch in the ocean?" Remove the three *Charlie* word cards and replace them with that child's name cards and add the sea creature that was chosen. Read or chant.

If you are using your children's names but did not print them, turn over the three *Charlie* word cards. Now, continue as described above, saying the child's name as your track the blank card.

6. Place all the words to the poem *Ocean, Ocean* in the pocket chart. Read or chant. (This will be chanted using the same meter as *Teddy Bear, Teddy Bear*) Discuss the word *ocean* and what the children think this word means. Bring out the globe and talk

about the blue areas representing the oceans. Ask the children if they can name any of the oceans. Use the globe to help the children locate the four main oceans – Atlantic, Pacific, Indian and Arctic.

7. Help the children identify the ocean that is nearest to their home. Place each of the four word cards printed with that ocean's name in the pocket chart as shown in the following picture:

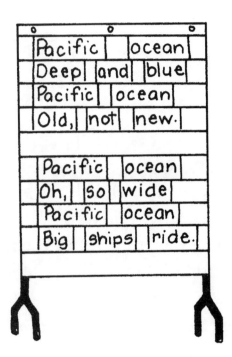

Read or chant. Repeat this procedure with each of the oceans.

8. If you wish to incorporate more writing, this is a wonderful poem to rewrite, either individually or as a class.
9. Introduce *Down By The Blue Sea* by reading the booklet you made after step 11 in Preparation. Read again, having the children chant, using the my turn, your turn technique.
10. The children sequence the pictures in the pocket chart, using your booklet as a guide, and chant as each picture is added.

Then, using phonetic clues, help the children match the appropriate word cards with each picture. Read. Give out all pictures and word cards. The children find their partners and place words and pictures back in the pocket chart.

11. Remove all items from the pocket chart. Help the children build the entire first verse, developing one line at a time.
Read and check for accuracy. Develop the remaining verses by changing the third line only. Place the new words directly on top of the old ones. By doing this, the children will have read this poem nine times and should be able to easily identify the words when it comes time for them to make their own individual booklets.

12. If your children need additional practice, distribute all the words from the first verse and have the children rebuild the poem, word by word, in the pocket chart.

Extension: *Individual Booklet*

We recommend that you have your children prepare the pages and the cover before you staple these pages into booklet form. We have tried to assemble this booklet several different ways and this is, by far, the easiest.

1. **Cover** – The cover, blackline 28, is colored and then glued to one piece of 6″ x 9″ dark blue construction paper.

2. **Pages** – The children cut waves from the 9″ x 3″ dark blue construction paper by gently scalloping one of the 9″ edges. Glue the three outside, straight edges to a piece of 9″ x 6″ light blue construction paper, thus creating a *pocket* for the various sea items. Repeat this for each of the nine pages.

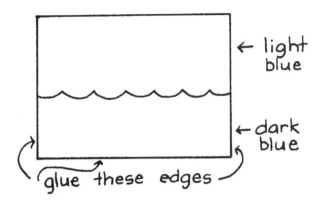

On two of these page glue a 1″ x 9″ piece of sandpaper to the bottom of the page, to represent the sand.

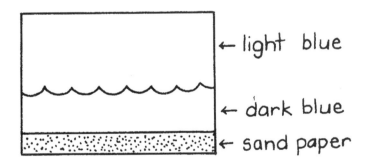

3. **Assembly** – Put the book together before the children add the pictures or the words. Assemble in the following manner: front cover, seven pages with waves, two pages with sandpaper added to the waves; and a back cover which is a piece of 9″ x 6″ dark blue construction paper. The teacher then staples these booklets together along the left hand edge.

4. **Pictures and words** – We suggest working on one verse at a time. The picture is colored, cut out and placed in the blue wave *pocket*. (**Note:** nothing goes behind the wave pocket on the sandy beach page.) The appropriate words are glued to the opposite page. For first grade, the children will copy each verse from the pocket chart or the chalkboard and glue in the same manner.

5. Read together and take home. An idea that was shared with us by a San Jose, California teacher (we are sorry that we don't know your name!) is for the child to read the booklet he has made to a parent and ask the parent to write a comment and sign her or his name. The books are then brought back to school and the comments are shared with the class.

Activity 5

Fish Eyes

Materials:

Materials needed:

- *Fish Eyes* by Lois Ehlert
- Five tongue depressors for stick puppets
- Contact paper or laminating film
- Felt pens
- Fine line felt pens for details on thumbprint fish
- Blacklines 33–37 for stick puppet fish
- Blacklines 38–40 for pocket chart pictures
- Blackline 41 for the cover of the *Fishy Facts* booklet
- Sentence strips
- Stamp pad (orange, red, green or black)
- 6″ x 9″ manila construction paper (lots!) for *Fishy Facts* booklets
- 6″ x 9″ yellow or orange construction paper for the booklet cover
- Goldfish crackers
- Paper plates or napkins
- To mount blacklines 38-40, you will need:
    — 5 pieces of 10½″ x 3½″ tagboard cards
    — 2 pieces of 6½″ x 3½″ tagboard cards
    — 2 pieces of 8½″ x 3½″ tagboard cards
    — 2 pieces of 4½″ x 3½″ tagboard cards

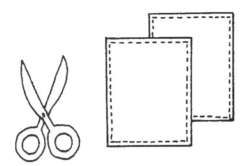

Preparation:

1. Duplicate blacklines 33-37 on 5 different colors of cardstock. Add features with felt pens. Cut and laminate or contact. Staple each fish puppet to a tongue depressor.

2. Color blacklines 38–40 (refer to *Fish Eyes* for ideas) and cut apart on the bold lines. Mount all eleven pictures on the appropriate size tagboard cards. Contact or laminate.

3. On sentence strips print the numerals *1–10*, a second numeral *1* card, a *plus* sign and an *equal* sign. Cut these apart and laminate or contact.

4. Refer to *Fish Eyes* and, on sentence strips, print the ten number phrases beginning with *one green fish* and ending with *ten darting fish.* Laminate or contact.

5. Duplicate blackline 41 on orange or yellow construction paper and cut in half. Each child will need one front cover. Cut plain orange or yellow construction paper for the back cover.

6. **Booklets**:

   Kindergarten Counting Booklet – We suggest that you prepare the booklets ahead of time. You will have a choice as to whether you want to prepare the pages with the numerals already printed on them or have the children write them. Staple five manila pages between the covers if you choose to work with the numerals 1–5 or staple ten pages if you wish to work with 1–10.

   First Grade Equation Booklet – We leave the choice to you as to whether you wish to prepare these booklets ahead of time or allow each child the opportunity to decide how many equation pages he/she will make. The covers will be added when the pages are completed.

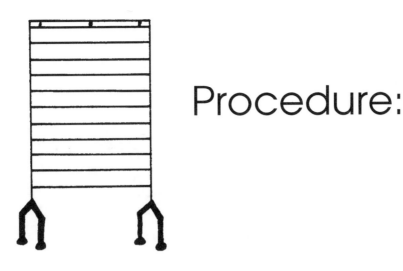

Procedure:

1. Introduce *5 Little Fishies* by holding up one of your hands and wiggling a different finger for each fishie as you chant the following:

   Five Little Fishies

   Five little fishies swimming in the sea,
   The 1st one said, "You can't see me!"
   The 2nd one said, "I'll race you to the bay."
   The 3rd one said, "Not now. I want to play!"
   The 4th one said, "It must be time to eat."
   The 5th one said, "A fishing boat! Good grief!!"

   Along came the fishing boat and dropped a line
   But the five little fishies swam away just in time!

2. Chant several times until most of the children are participating. Discuss the vocabulary. Depending on the time of year, you may need to work with ordinal numbers a bit.

3. Dramatize by having all the children take the parts of all five fish and the fishing boat. This is a bit noisy but very effective in developing meaning.

4. Distribute the five stick puppets to five children. As the class chants the poem, each *fishie* solos with the appropriate response ("You can't see me!", etc.). Continue until each child has a turn.

5. Introduce the book, *Fish Eyes* by Lois Ehlert. We suggest taking the book jacket off before reading this book to the children as it has a picture of the little guide fish that we like to *accidentally discover* on the inside back cover.

6. Initially read only the words in white print. Enjoy the brilliant illustrations and help the children predict what the next numeral will be. When you reach the inside back cover (where the little gray fish says, "Good-bye! Hope to see you again.") feign surprise and help the children trace him back to the beginning of the book. Now reread the story (including both black and white print), enjoying the little fish's comments and helping the class solve the addition equations.

7. Have the children help you sequence the numerals 1–10 along the left side of the pocket chart. Display the pictures from blacklines 38–40 at random along the right side of the pocket chart. Help the children match each group of fish with the appropriate numeral. Count for accuracy.

8. For younger children you may wish to only work with the numerals and the pictures. Distribute the numeral cards as well as the picture cards. The children find their partners and rebuild the 1–10 sequence in the pocket chart.

9. Using the book as a guide, place each phrase card by the appropriate picture. Chant or read all the lines that are in the pocket chart each time you add a new phrase. For older children you will want to distribute the phrase cards along with the picture and numeral cards. The children would rebuild in the same manner and read or chant to check for accuracy.

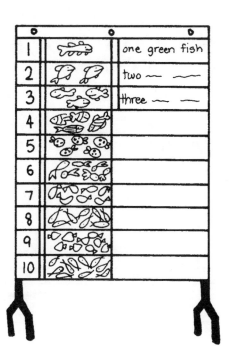

Extension:

Fishy Facts Booklets

Note: If you are going to do the Kindergarten Booklet, steps 1–5 are not necessary.

1. Give each child a paper plate (or a napkin, blue construction paper, etc.) and ten goldfish crackers.

2. Reread the first equation in the book, *Fish Eyes*, (both white and black print). However, omit the answer. Have the children create this first equation with their fish crackers. The children chant the equation and *count on* to arrive at the answer. (1 + 1 = 2)

   Help the children rebuild this equation using the pocket chart pictures along with the little card that has a plus sign, little fish and equal sign. The children, after *counting on* to arrive at the correct sum, then place the appropriate picture to complete the equation. Read from the pocket chart.

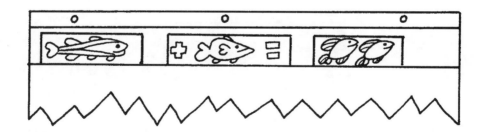

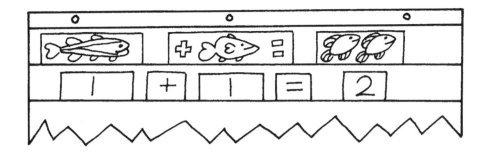

Lastly, help the children find the numerals and symbols that represent this equation and place these in the pocket chart directly below the pictures. Read again.

3. Follow this same procedure for each equation.

4. Now the children may take turns creating their own equations. One at a time, a child builds an equation with his crackers and the remainder of the class duplicates this equation with their crackers. Then the child builds the equation in the pocket chart using both pictures and symbols. The class reads this equation from the pocket chart.

5. **Kindergarten *Fishy Facts* Booklet** – Distribute the prepared booklets to the class. If your children are going to write the numerals, help them sequentially write one numeral per page.

Illustrations for each page are made by creating thumbprint fish. We suggest using ink pads but tempra will also work. It is much easier to have the children make all the thumbprints for the entire booklet at one time. If you have never experienced thumb-print pictures, you may wish to refer to Ed Emberley's book, *Great Thumbprint Drawing Book.* After the ink or paint has dried, the children use fine line felt pens to add details.

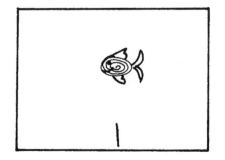
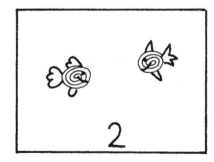

If you wish, the children could add ocean and seaweed.

6. **First Grade *Fishy Facts* Booklet** – Each child will build their own equations with the crackers and record the equations (one equation per page) on each of the booklet pages. The children are now ready to illustrate each equation using thumbprint fish. See above step for directions. These need to be created so that there are distinct groupings to represent each equation that is recorded.

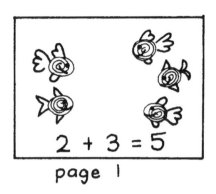

page 1

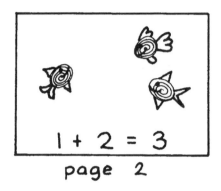

page 2

We strongly suggest that sums be no larger than ten as the pages become much too cluttered and busy and therefore, difficult to count.

Scenery (ocean, seaweed, etc.) is fun to add. When completed the children may wish to read their equation booklet to a friend.

And...this is a good time to introduce your children to "The Whale Game" in *Mathematics Their Way*, by Mary Baratta-Lorton, pages 188–189.

In Addition... Patricia MacCarthy has a great counting book called *Ocean Parade*. The batik artwork makes this book a real treat.

Also...another book that addresses both numbers and equations is *Sea Squares* by Joy N. Hulme. Although this book does develop the squares of numbers it also lends itself to primary grades and serial addition.

Activity 6

Octopus

Materials:

Materials needed:

- *Herman the Helper* by Robert Kraus
- *Octopus* by Charlotte Diamond (big book)
- *10 Carrot Diamond* by Charlotte Diamond (record or tape)
- Any factual book containing information about an octopus
- Blacklines 42–43 of octopus body and arms for the extension
- Chart paper
- Felt pens
- Laminating film or contact paper

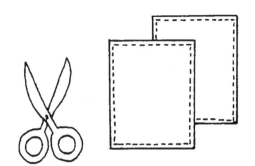

Preparation:

1. Print the poem, *Fish* by Mary Ann Hoberman, on chart paper.

Fish

Look at them flit
Lickety–split
Wiggling
Swiggling
Swerving
Curving
Hurrying
Scurrying
Chasing
Racing
Whizzing
Whisking
Flying
Frisking
Tearing around
With a leap and a bound
But none of them making the tiniest
                          tiniest
                 tiniest
         tiniest
sound.

You may wish to have the children illustrate, add colorful sea stickers, etc.

2. Duplicate blackline 42 on colored construction paper. Cut in half. Each child will need one body.

3. Duplicate blackline 43 on the same color of construction that was used for the body. Each child will need eight arms.

4. For a kindergarten or beginning first grade class book, prepare the following blackline masters. You will need to duplicate about twenty-five of **A** and nine of **B**.

5. Color and laminate or contact the big book, *Octopus.*

6. You may need to do some research on the octopus. Most factual books dealing with sea creatures include at least one page about the octopus. If you have difficulty locating references, below are some basic facts:

  – has eight tentacles (sometimes called legs or arms)
  – has two eyes
  – can move by shooting out a stream of water
  – can change colors
  – can shoot out a dark fluid to hide from enemies
  – has three hearts
  – can eat shellfish, fish and mollusks
  – has no bones
  – can grow a new tentacle if one is cut off
  – can breathe by means of gills
  – can lay eggs
  – can be both small and large
  – has a highly developed brain
  – can be rather shy and not aggressive

Procedure:

1. Read the poem, *Fish,* by Mary Ann Hoberman.
2. Read the poem again, asking the children to listen for the rhyming words. Help the children find the rhyming words on the chart.
3. Use dramatization to help develop the language of the poem. The children will use one hand for the fish and enact each movement in the poem. Depending on the proximity of your principals office to your classroom, you may wish to let the children use their whole body to dramatize the movements. Just remember that over half of these movements are quite rapid actions!
4. Read the poem again, with the children joining in where they are able. Ask the children to think of other ways that fish can move. Be sure to include the following: *sliding, squigilling, splashing, lurking* and *spouting.* (These words will be found in the song, *Octopus.*) Discuss and dramatize each word.
5. Introduce the song *Octopus* by using the big book along with the tape or record, tracking the words as you sing. The children will be joining in after just a few stanzas. Be sure the volume on your record or tape player is adequate as there is a surprise at the end of this song! Your children will really love this song and will beg to sing it all year long.
6. Ask the children to tell you everything they know about the octopus. Discuss these ideas. Tell the children you are going to read about the octopus. You want them to listen very carefully because when you are finished you are going to ask them to try

46

to remember all the things they learned that this sea creature **can do**. Read factual information about the octopus.

7. After reading factual information about the octopus, divide the chalkboard or large paper in half. Label one side **"An octopus can _____"** and label the other side **"But, an octopus can not _____."** Brainstorm for all the things an octopus can do and record.

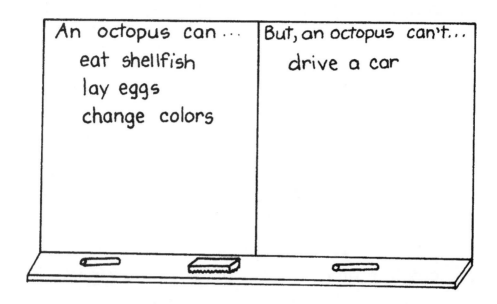

8. Chant or read all the brainstorming. (An octopus can eat shellfish. An octopus can lay eggs. etc.) Brainstorm for things that an octopus can't do and chant these ideas (An octopus can't drive a car. An octopus can't read. etc.)

9. Orally develop several contrasts by using the following frame:

   An octopus can _____.
   An octopus can _____.
   An octopus can _____.
   But, an octopus can't _____.

10. You may wish to give your children a short directed drawing lesson on how to illustrate an octopus. If you need ideas, please refer to *Ed Emberley's Drawing Book of Animals*.

11. The children are now ready to write a class book. We have had success using the following procedure:
    – Ask a child to tell you what an octopus **can** do and give that child a blank piece of white paper (**Note:** Kindergarten and beginning first grade children will use the pages you prepared in step 4 under Preparation.)
    – Instruct this child to print, "An octopus can _____." Using the brainstorming as a reference the child then completes the frame and illustrates the page.
    – Repeat this step two more times with a second and third child.
    – Ask a fourth child to tell you something that an octopus **can't** do. This child completes the writing, using the frame, "An octopus can't _____." and adds the illustrations.
    – Continue in this manner until each child has a page to complete. We like to use this procedure because we are insured that there will be a variety of ideas. Also, we can regulate the can/can't sentences to create the contrasts.
    – Have the children help make a cover. Bind the pages and cover into a class book entitled, "An Octopus Can..." Add this to your class library.
    – You might wish to make another class book entitled, "An Octopus Has..."

Note: Another idea is for each child to make his or her own four-page booklet. We like to make small sized booklets and let each child choose their own ideas from the brainstorming.

Extension:

1. Read *Herman the Helper* by Robert Kraus. Discuss the ways that Herman helped everyone.

2. Brainstorm and list on the chalkboard ways that the children are able to help their family and friends.

3. Distribute the body and arms from blacklines 42–43. The children print their name on the body on the appropriate line. Using the brainstorming as a guide, the children print one way in which they can help on each tentacle. Depending upon ability, you may wish to take dictation or have the children copy from the chalkboard. (You may wish to only have the children complete a few of the arms and take the octopus home where more helpful ideas may be added.)

4. The children now cut the arms and body and assemble – either by gluing, stapling or by using brads.

Activity 7

Mr. Gumpy's Outing

 Materials:

Materials Needed:

- *Mr. Gumpy's Outing* by John Burningham
- *Who Sank The Boat?* by Pamela Allen
- *Mr. Little's Noisy Boat* by Richard Fowler
- Blacklines 44–46 for pocket chart pictures
- 9 pieces of 5″ x 6″ tagboard cards for the pocket chart
- Objects for sink or float lesson (rock, wooden block, scissors, bar of Ivory soap, bar of regular soap, wooden spoon, crayon, ruler, coins, piece of paper, etc.)
- Large tub (clear if you can find one) for the sink or float lesson
- Blackline 47 for class book
- Sentence strips
- Felt pens
- Contact paper or laminating film

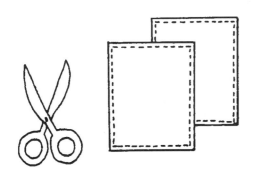

Preparation:

1. Color, cut and mount blacklines 44–46 on 5″ x 6″ tagboard cards. Contact or laminate.

2. Print on sentence strips the following songs:

Row, row, row your boat,	**Propel, propel, propel your craft,**
Gently down the stream,	**Down the liquid solution,**
Merrily, merrily,	**Ecstatically, ecstatically,**
Merrily, merrily,	**Ecstatically, ecstatically,**
Life is but a dream.	**Existence is but an illusion.**

For steps 3 and 4: For ease in matching, you may wish to use a different color for each animal and the directions the animal was given. For example, *children* and *don't squabble* would both be printed in red felt pen.

3. On sentence strips, print the following and cut into individual word cards:

children	**rabbit**	**cat**
dog	**pig**	**sheep**
chickens	**calf**	**goat**

4. Refer to *Mr. Gumpy's Outing* for the direction each animal was given and print these words on sentence strips. (don't squabble, don't hop, etc.)

5. Duplicate blackline 47, one per child, for a class book.

6. Prepare a sink or float lesson. (You need a tub and sink or float items)

Procedure:

1. Introduce this lesson by reading *Mr. Little's Noisy Boat* by Richard Fowler. We have been told at present this book is out of print. Please check your library – any book dealing with the parts of a boat will do nicely. This is a funny story that includes many facts about the parts of a boat.

2. Place the words to *Row, Row, Row Your Boat* in the pocket chart. Sing, tracking the words in the pocket chart as you go along. Ask the children what the words in the first line mean. Many of the children may not know what a row boat is and how the oars are used.

3. Continue in this manner until you have developed the language of this poem. (merrily, gently, life, dream, stream)

4. Now tell the children you know another way to sing this song using really *fancy* words. Place the words for this second version in the pocket chart next to the original song. Sing. Ask the children if they can figure out what "Propel, propel, propel your craft" means. Continue in this manner with each line until the entire song is developed.

5. Another way to develop this song is to place the new words directly on top of the original words. Sing, encouraging the children to join in as they learn the words. You may wish to add hand motions as you sing. This is fun as a round but difficult with small children. It is a great song to sing as an *echo,* using one version to echo the other. (Row, row, row your boat – Propel, propel, propel your craft.)

6. Tell the children that you have a story, called *Mr. Gumpy's Outing.* It is about a scow which is very much like a row boat. Read and enjoy the story. Discuss the reason that things went wrong – passengers don't behave as they are told.

7. Read the story again, telling the children to listen for the names of all the passengers. Now ask the class to tell you all the characters they can remember. As the children name each passenger, place that picture in the pocket chart. Using the book as a reference, help the children sequence these characters in the pocket chart.

8. Using phonetic clues, help the children match each picture with the appropriate word card. Chant or read. Working with the pocket chart, line by line, ask the children to try to remember what Mr. Gumpy said to each character before they got in the boat. Add the appropriate text to each line and reread. Refer back to the book if help is needed.

	children	don't squabble
	rabbit	don't hop
	cat	
	dog	
	pig	
	sheep	
	chickens	
	calf	
	goat	

9. Chant or read the completed pocket chart. Now distribute all twenty-seven cards to the class and have the children find their partners and replace the cards in the pocket chart. Read or chant to check for accuracy.

10. This story is a must for dramatization! If you act out this *play* three times, each child will have a turn **or** you may wish to have each child pretend to be each animal and the teacher or a capable student could be Mr. Gumpy.

11. Read *Who Sank The Boat?* by Pamela Allen. Compare and contrast this with *Mr. Gumpy's Outing*. How are these stories alike? How are they different? In which boat would you like to ride? You might like to make a graph to discover the favorite of the class.

Extension:

Class Book and Sink or Float Lesson

Class Book:

1. Discuss who the children would invite if they had their own boat. How many passengers would your boat hold? Would you ask any animals?

2. Distribute blackline 47 to each child. The children print their name at the bottom (Miriam's boat). Illustrate and label all the passengers in the boat. You may need to take dictation if the children are younger.

3. First grade children can write a short story about the passengers that are on their boat. Be sure to brainstorm for directions that might be given – don't stand up, no jump ropes allowed, don't chew gum, etc.

4. Bind together with a cover and add a title such as *Our Outings*. Read and add to your class library.

Sink or Float:

1. Fill a fairly large see-through tub with water.

2. If needed, develop the vocabulary *sink* and *float*.

3. Before placing each item you have gathered in the tub, have the children predict whether the items will sink or float.

4. After trying each item, help the children decide whether more of the objects sank or more of the objects floated. If the answer is not obvious, you may wish to do an informal graph by lining the objects up and matching them one to one.

5. For additional activities, you may wish to use AIMS materials, 1984 Project AIMS. We like the activities *Floating Fruit, Blue Wave* and *What Do You Sink Will Float.*

6. You may also wish to have the children make boats and see if they will sink or float.

Activity 8

What's In The Deep Blue Sea?

Materials:

Materials needed:

- *What's In The Deep Blue Sea?* by Peter Seymore
- Factual books that discuss sea environments, such as:
    - *When The Tide is Low* by Shelia Cole
    - *Whales and Sharks and Other Creatures of the Deep* by Susanne Miller
    - *Giant Sea Creatures* by Edith Kunhardt
- Wordbank pictures (at least sixty)
- White butcher paper for stuffed sea creatures
- Tempra paints – all colors
- Newsprint for stuffing
- Reference books with large pictures of sea animals
- Sentence strips
- Felt pens

Preparation:

1. On sentence strips print the following:

| A _____ lives in a tide pool. |
| An _____ lives in a tide pool. |
| A _____ lives in shallow water. |
| An _____ lives in shallow water. |
| A _____ lives on the shoreline. |
| An _____ lives on the shoreline. |

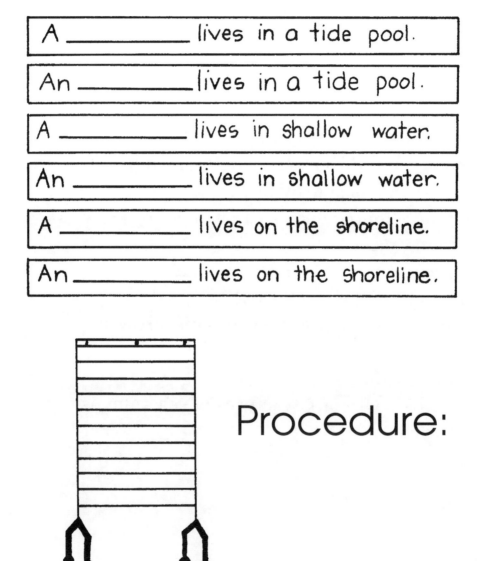

Procedure:

1. Read the wonderful pop-up book, *What's in the Deep Blue Sea?*
   Discuss the vocabulary and words such as *lurking, squiggly,*

jiggly and *shy*. Read the book again and see if the children are able to remember where all the creatures were hiding.

2. Dramatize each creature's actions. Read again, letting the children join in where they are able.

3. Ask the questions, "Do all the creatures that we just read about live in the same part of the sea that a whale does? Do you know what part of the sea would be their home?"

4. We have listed three factual books that we like to use at this time. We chose these books because they are written in language that is appropriate for very young children. We recommend you use these books or similar ones that deal with the various habitats of the ocean in which sea animals are found.

   Begin by reading sections from the factual books that include information about animals that live in the tide pools, shallow water and along the shore line.

   Another source for information is *Sea Animals* from *Come With Me Science Series*. This unit addresses lobsters, squids, seahorses, starfish and hermit crabs.

5. Using a set of sea animal cards, sort and classify by whether or not the animal lives by the edge of the ocean. Divide your class into groups of 4–6 and give each group about fifteen animal cards. (For this reason, you will need about sixty cards. You may wish to make duplicate sets for each group.) Ask the children to make three piles:

   1. Animals that live at the edge of the ocean
   2. Animals that don't live at the edge of the ocean
   3. I don't know

6. Each group brings all three stacks and places them by the pocket chart.

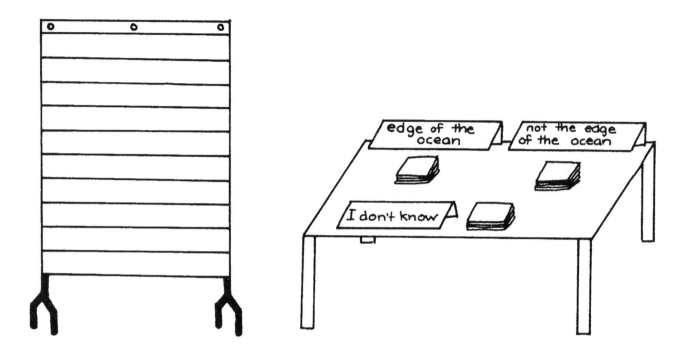

7. At this point, discuss the animals that are in the *I don't know* pile. The class works together to decide into which pile to put the animals. If no one knows, use your reference books to solve the problem.

8. Check for accuracy by reviewing each of the sorted animal cards. You may wish to have the children show a thumbs up sign for yes and thumbs down for no. Save the sea animals that don't live at the edge of the ocean for further sorting. (see step 11)

9. In the pocket chart place all the pictures of the animals that live at the edge of the ocean. Chant, "A starfish lives at the edge of the ocean. A crab lives at the edge of the ocean." etc. **Note:** You may need to discuss with your class the meaning of tide pool, shallow water and shoreline.

10. Using the reference books as a guide, help the children decide which of these animals live in the tide pools, which live in the shallow water and which live on the shore line. Place the prepared sentence strips in the pocket chart. Let the children take turns

choosing animal pictures to put in the blanks and chant or read.

11. On additional days, you will need to continue this lesson to include animals that live in the open sea and animals that live down deep. We suggest that you follow steps 4–9 for each of the two remaining categories.

 Extension: *Stuffed Sea Creatures and Sea Habitats Bulletin Board*

Stuffed Sea Creatures:

1. Each child needs a piece of butcher paper measuring 6' x 3'. Fold this in half so it measures about 3' x 3'. (This may be too large for some creatures so you may wish to offer smaller paper also.)

2. Using reference books or pocket chart pictures as guides, the children choose a sea creature and sketch it with a pencil. Encourage the children to make these animals as large as the paper allows. Before cutting the sea creatures, be sure the two layers of butcher paper are stapled together in several places.

3. After the child cuts the creature, he/she staples the two layers of butcher paper together, being careful to leave an opening for the stuffing.

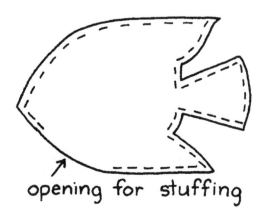
opening for stuffing

4. Children use small pieces of wadded up newsprint for the stuffing. Staple the opening closed. Using the pictures (reference books or pocket chart pictures) as a guide, the children paint one side of their sea creature. After drying, the other side will be painted. Features may be added with paint or with wide felt tip pens. Add string or yarn and hang from the ceiling, light fixtures or wires.

You may wish to drape a large fish net over a wire or staple it to a wall. Hanging blue and green crepe paper streamers is very effective also.

Sea Habitats Bulletin Board:

If you choose to make a bulletin board you will need:

> blue butcher paper
> white butcher paper
> black butcher paper
> tan paint
> black paint
> blue paint
> white paint
> small sponges
> large grey construction paper

1. Cover your bulletin board with blue butcher paper everywhere except where the down deep section will be. Cover that section with black butcher paper.

2. On large sections of white butcher paper, sponge paint the following: blue for the waves, tan for the shoreline, black for deep waves and *light* blue for the tide pool. When the sponge paint is dry, cut three inch wavy strips from the blue and black. Be sure to cut both edges *wavy*.

3. For the tan shoreline, make your strip about 9" wide and cut a wavy line on one edge only. The straight edge will be the bottom of your bulletin board.

4. To make a tide pool, cut a free-form shape from the light blue sponge painted butcher paper. Cut rocks from grey construction paper and place in and around the tide pool.

5. Use the following illustration for placement of the waves, shoreline, tide pool and rocks.

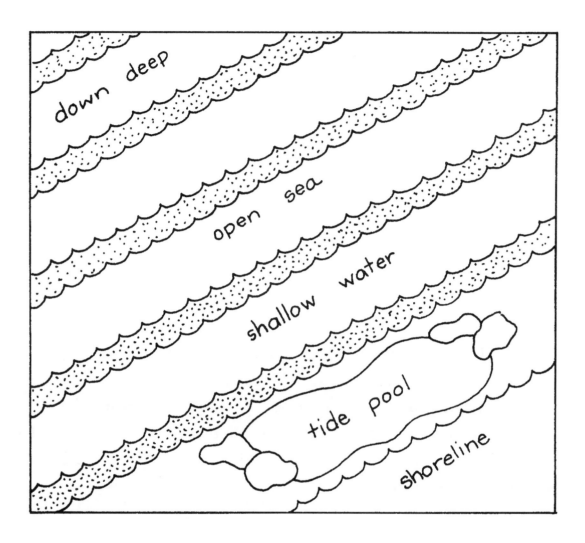

6. Label the habitats if you wish.
7. Each child chooses a sea creature to paint. After the paint is dry,
you may wish to outline with a wide felt tip pen and then have
the child cut out the sea animal. When everyone has made an
animal for the bulletin board, ask the children to bring their animal picture and sit in a large circle. Working together, the class
sorts the animals by habitat and then they are placed in the
appropriate habitat on the bulletin board.

Activity 9

One, One, The Beach Is Fun

Materials:

Materials needed:

- *One, One, The Beach Is Fun* by Margaret Banks (big book)
- Pocket chart pictures (included with the big book)
- *Ed Emberley's Picture Pie* by Ed Emberley
- Blackline 48 for booklet cover
- Blackline 49 for art project (kindergarten)
- Blackline 50 for the pocket chart
- 4 pieces of 5" x 6" tagboard cards for the pocket chart
- Sentence strips
- Felt pens
- 9" x 12" light blue construction paper (One per child)
- Various colors of construction paper for the fish
- Two or three shades of green tissue paper
- Liquid starch
- Large paint brushes
- Contact paper or laminating film
- Lined writing paper (first grade)
- Drinking cups to trace

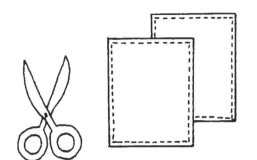

Preparation:

1. Duplicate three copies of blackline 48 on white construction paper for the covers of the class books.
2. Color the big book and the pocket chart pictures from *One, One, The Beach Is Fun.* Contact or laminate.
3. Print on sentence strips the following:

> **1,2,3,4,5,**
> **I caught a fish alive,**
> **6,7,8,9,10,**
> **I let it go again.**
>
> **Why did you let it go?**
> **Because it bit my finger so.**
> **Which finger did it bite?**
> **This little finger on the right.**

Cut the first four lines into individual word cards, leaving the last four lines in complete strips.

4. For kindergarten: Using assorted colors of construction paper, duplicate one copy of blackline 49 for every two children. Cut apart on the dotted lines. Each child will need two complete circles of different colors. **Note:** First grade will trace drinking cups, fold into quarters, and cut.

5. Color, cut and mount or contact blackline 50 on 5" x 6" tagboard cards. Laminate or contact.

6. Cut the various shades of green tissue paper into 9" x 4" strips – each child will need one strip of each color.

7. On sentence strips print the text from *One, One, The Beach Is Fun.* We suggest you print each of the ten pages in a different color for ease in rebuilding the entire text. Cut the sentence strips into individual word cards.

8. Print the numerals 1–10 and the number words one–ten on sentence strips. Cut apart into individual cards.

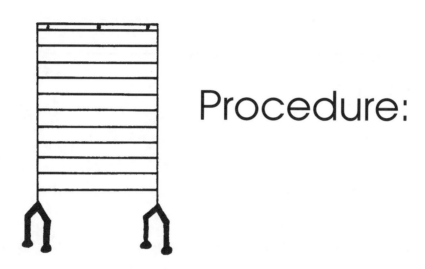

Procedure:

1. Chant the poem, *One, Two, Three, Four, Five* as you place the four pictures (from blackline 50) in sequential order in the pocket chart. **Note:** When you place these pictures in the pocket chart, be sure to skip a line between each picture. Chant two or three more times, having the children join in when they are able.

2. The children place the numerals 1–5 in the first line and 6–10 in the third line of the pocket chart. Have the children help you place the remaining word cards (of the first verse) in the pocket chart. Chant or read.

3. Add the second verse, written on strips, to the pocket chart and read or chant several times.

4. Tell the children that you have another book with numbers but they are written differently. Place the numerals 1–10 in the pocket chart, one numeral to a pocket. Using beginning and ending sounds as clues, have the children help you match the number words to the numeral cards. Read.

1	one		
2	two		
3	three		
4	four		
5	five		
6	six		
7	seven		
8	eight		
9	nine		
10	ten		

5. Distribute all numeral and number word cards to the children and have them find their partners and rebuild the sequence in the pocket chart. Read to check for accuracy. We find that step 4 and step 5 are necessary preliminary activities for the big book, *One, One, The Beach Is Fun.* (Before continuing, be sure to remove the numeral and number word cards from the pocket chart.)

6. Read and enjoy the big book, *One, One, The Beach Is Fun.* Help the children sequentially place the individual number words in the pocket chart. Read or chant the entire book again, having the children join in on the number words as you track them in the pocket chart.

one	one	
two	two	
three	three	
four	four	
five	five	
six	six	
seven	seven	
eight	eight	
nine	nine	
ten	ten	

7. Read again, listening for the rhyming words. Turn to the pocket chart, read and track the words, "One, one," and ask the children to tell you what word rhymes with *one* and then insert the appropriate picture on the far right side of the pocket chart. Continue doing this until the entire set of rhyming words have been developed. If the children have difficulty remembering some of the rhyming words, have them use the book as a reference. Now ask the children to chant the entire book, using the pocket chart as a guide.

(Kindergarten may wish to skip step eight as there are a significant number of words in the remaining text.)

8. Ask the children to chant the rhymes again as you add the remaining words for each line. Read from the pocket chart. Because each line is color coded, this book is easily rebuilt. Simply distribute all word cards and pictures and have the children rebuild the book. Read to check for accuracy.

9. This book is a must for a rewrite. To prepare for this, the children will need to create a rhyming wordbank. Write the number words **one – ten** across the top of your chalkboard. Help the class list words that rhyme with each number.

one	two	three	four	five	six	seven	eight	nine	ten
sun	blue	me	more						
run	boo	see							
bun	who	flea							
ton	do	tree							
done	you	she							
fun									

10. Orally help the children create a number of rhyming couplets, referring to the rhyming wordbank for ideas. You may have to help the children with the meter by clapping the rhythm to assist them with either adding or deleting words or syllables. (One, one, playing in the sun. One, one, hot dog on a bun. One, one, the day is done.)

11. It is not absolutely necessary that the children's ideas are recorded in a class book, but we like to do so. Because each child will want to participate in making a page and there are only ten pages, you will need to make three books. It does not matter if some of the same couplets are in each book.

Kindergarten: for a class of thirty you will need thirty pieces of 9″ x 12″ white construction paper. We suggest you prepare the booklet pages ahead of time. Make three copies of the first two words of each page (One, one, – Two, two, etc.). This will shorten the time you spend taking the children's dictation.

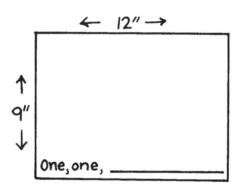

Ask the children, "Who would like one? Two?" etc., choosing three children for each number. Call each child up individually and quickly record their choice from the rhyming wordbank. The child illustrates. Volunteers may color the three covers and then the pages are collated and three individual books are created.

First Grade: follow the same format as above, only the children will write their own couplets, using the rhyming wordbank as a reference, rather than the teacher taking dictation.

71

Extension: *Circle Fish Art*

1. Kindergarten will be using circles from blackline 49 while first grade children will need to trace two circles, using paper drinking cups (about 3″ in diameter).

2. The method for creating these circle fish is found in *Ed Emberley's Picture Pie – a circle drawing book.* You may have your own favorite idea of making paper fish but we find this is so simple that all children have success.

3. The children glue the two fish on 9″ x 12″ light blue construction paper.

4. Distribute a 9″ x 4″ strip of each shade of green tissue paper to every child. The children use their fingers and gently tear strips of seaweed from the tissue and place it on the construction paper, creating a seascape. Do not glue!

5. To complete this art project, the children will dip a paintbrush in liquid starch and, using vertical strokes, carefully cover the entire paper. The tissue paper will become translucent as it dries and the overall effect will be of fish swimming through seaweed.

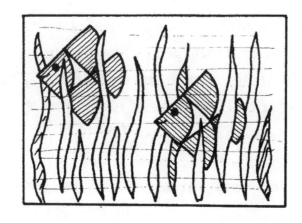

Activity 10

Five Silly Fishermen

 Materials:

Materials needed:

- *Four Brave Sailors* by Mirra Ginsburg
- *Five Silly Fishermen* by Roberta Edwards
- Sentence strips
- Blacklines 51–52 for the pocket chart
- 8 pieces of 5" x 6" tagboard cards for the pocket chart
- Blacklines 53–56 for Make a Play
- 12" x 18" light blue construction paper, one per child
- 9" x 12" dark blue construction paper, one per child
- Felt tip pens
- Contact paper or laminating film
- Yarn

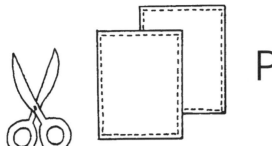

Preparation:

1. Color, cut and mount blacklines 51–52 on 5″ x 6″ tagboard cards. Laminate or contact.
2. Duplicate blackline 33 on dark blue construction paper for the water. **Note:** Cut on the dotted line to separate the two sections of water. Each child will need only one section.
3. Fold the 12″ x 18″ light blue construction paper in half so it measures 9″ x 12″, one per child.
4. Duplicate blacklines 54–56, one per child, of the make-a-play characters. Cut apart on the bold lines.
5. On sentence strips print the following:

   fisherman 1
   fisherman 2
   fisherman 3
   fisherman 4
   fisherman 5
   little girl

   Punch holes in the upper two corners of each sentence strip and attach a piece of yarn that is large enough to slip over the children's heads.
6. On sentence strips, print the *Long-Legged Sailor.*

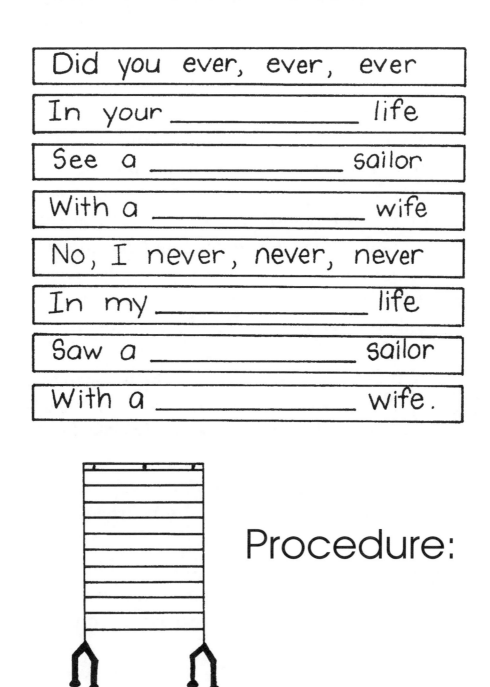

Did you ever, ever, ever

In your _____ life

See a _____ sailor

With a _____ wife

No, I never, never, never

In my _____ life

Saw a _____ sailor

With a _____ wife.

Procedure:

1. Read *Four Brave Sailors*, enjoying the fantasy and the surprise ending. Discuss the sea life the four brave sailors saw. How do the children know that this was just a dream? Return to the first page and help the children find there was a second shelf in the room that held the polar bear, penguin and pirate. Do you think there was a third shelf? What might be on that third shelf?

2. The sailors in the book were brave. Discuss the meaning of the word brave. Tell the children you are going to teach them a song about some sailors – this time the sailors are funny. Place the sentence strips from *Long-Legged Sailor* in the pocket chart. Display the first picture (long-legged) in the pocket chart, next to the text.

3. Sing the first verse (tune: *Turkey In The Straw*), tracking as you go. Be sure to point to the picture, singing *long-legged*, each time you come to a blank space. We chose to work the pocket chart in this manner but you could make six copies of each picture or print the text six times (for each verse) and place those in each blank.

   Continue in this manner with each of the following verses: short-legged, knock-kneed, bow-egged, cross-eyed, bald-headed, big-eared and buck-toothed. You may need to develop meaning on some of these.

4. Now brainstorm for other attributes to fit in the structure. (Flat-footed, pigeon-toed, patch-eyed, red-bearded, etc.)

   Note: It should be remembered that this is an old traditional campfire song and is not intended to poke fun at anyone. The children always enjoy the nonsense of this song.

5. Moving from funny fishermen to silly fishermen is the next step. Tell the children you are going to read a story called *Five Silly Fishermen*. Discuss the meaning of the word silly. Ask the children to listen to the story and be ready to tell what made these fishermen silly. (We would prefer to use the book *Six Foolish Fishermen* but it is, sadly, out of print at this time. If you are one of the lucky ones that has a copy, you may wish to use it instead. You will need one more fisherman and a boy for the make-a-play.)

6. Read and enjoy the book, *Five Foolish Fishermen*. Discuss the foolishness of these fishermen.

7. This book is a must for drama, not only for pure enjoyment but also to clarify the utter nonsense for the less sophisticated child. Choose six children for the characters and let each one wear the appropriate label. Read the story again, helping the children with the actions. (We do not use props but they are easily added.) Select six more children to enact the play again and continue in this manner until all the children in your class have had a turn. By the third or fourth dramatization, the children should be able to join in with the narration. By the last performance, the children should have the story and the sequences memorized.

Extension:

Make-A-Play

Begin with the water. This will not only be the backdrop but also be used as a storage area for all the characters of this play. Cut the dark blue water (blackline 53). Open up the large 12″ x 18″ light blue construction paper folder. If you open the folder, the children are less apt to try to glue the water upside down! Carefully glue around the sides and bottom of the water, being sure not to glue the top. Glue the water to the paper folder, matching the corners at the bottom. You have now created a storage pocket. Using crayons, have the children illustrate clouds, sun, birds, etc., at the top.

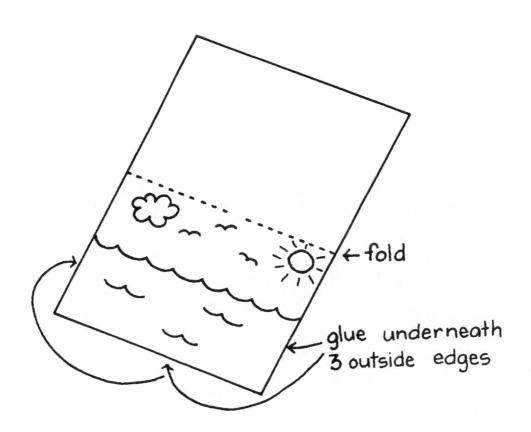

← fold

glue underneath
3 outside edges

Color the five fishermen and the little girl (blacklines 54–56). Carefully fold on the dotted lines. Be sure to tell your children **not to cut** the individual fishermen as they do not stand as well as the larger rectangles.

When completed, stand up the folder and place the fishermen and the girl behind it. Now the children are ready to retell the story, using the characters to dramatize the action–thus, making-a-play. They will particularly enjoy having each character jump into the water at the end of the story.

Before taking home, have the children place all of the characters in the pocket behind the water and close the folder.

79

Activity 11

A House For Hermit Crab

 Materials:

Materials needed:

- *A House For Hermit Crab* by Eric Carle
- *Is This a House for Hermit Crab?* by Megan McDonald
- *Kermit the Hermit* by Bill Peet
- Blackline 57 is a large picture of hermit crab
- Blacklines 58–59 for pocket chart pictures (McDonald book)
- Blacklines 60–62 for pocket chart pictures (Carle book) and stocking cap activity

   Note: For the stocking cap activity you will need to enlarge Blacklines 58–62.
- Blacklines 63–64 for the art project
- Child's stocking cap
- Velcro **or** double-sided tape
- 12″ x 18″ light blue or white construction paper
- Sponges for sponge painting
- Finger paint
- Paper for finger painting
- Sentence strips
- Felt tip pens
- Contact paper or laminating film
- 18 pieces of 5″ x 6″ tagboard cards for the pocket chart

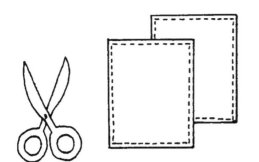

Preparation:

1. Color blackline 57. Mount and contact or laminate.
2. Color blacklines 58–59 for the pocket chart. Cut apart and mount on 5″ x 6″ tagboard cards. Contact or laminate.
3. Use blacklines 60–62 to **enlarge** the following on stiff cardstock: sea anemone, starfish, coral, snails, sea urchin, seaweed, lantern fish and pebbles. Color, cut and laminate or contact. Attach a small piece of velcro or double sided tape to the back of each of these **except** for the seaweed, lantern fish and pebbles.
4. If you used velcro in step 3, attach five matching pieces of velcro to a stocking cap.

5. Color, cut apart and mount blacklines 60–62 on 5″ x 6″ tagboard cards. Contact or laminate.
6. Duplicate blackline 63–64 on white construction paper, one per child.
7. Print the names of the months of the year (January–December) on sentence strips. Cut apart into individual word cards.

8. Print the following on individual word cards:

rock	**too heavy**
tin can	**too noisy**
driftwood	**too dark**
pail	**too deep**
hole	**too crowded**
fishing net	**too many holes**
sea snail shell	**just right**

9. On a sentence strip, print the following:

**So he stepped along the shore, by the sea, in the sand...
scritch-scratch, scritch-scratch**

10. On individual word cards print the following:

Gently   Carefully   Gingerly   Happily   Gratefully

11. On a sentence strip print the following:

**_____, Hermit Crab picked it up with
his claw and placed it on his shell.**

12. You may need to do some research on the hermit crab.
    If you cannot find information in the factual books you have,
    here are a few characteristics. Hermit crabs:
    - are found on beaches and in oceans all over the world
    - live in tide pools, on the ocean floor or on land
    - are crustaceans that do not grow their own complete shell
    - eat small sea animals
    - are good fighters
    - have a soft unprotected rear part, making it necessary for
      them to find a shell in which to reside
    - continuously outgrow their shells and look for new ones
    - protect themselves by withdrawing inside the shell and
      sealing the opening of the shell with their tough claws

Procedure:

1. Show the children a picture of a hermit crab. We like to use a photograph from a book or magazine but if you cannot locate one large enough, use the illustration on blackline 57. Ask the children if they have ever heard about or seen such a creature. Talk about the various attributes and draw particular attention to the soft unprotected rear-section of this creature. Discuss the name hermit crab and what it means.

2. Discuss the fact that the hermit crab is different from all other crabs. Ask them to listen as you read or tell factual information about the hermit crab and see if they can tell you how the hermit crab is different from other crabs. **Note:** You may need to give the children additional information about crabs in general if you have not done so already.

3. Tell the children that you have a special story about a hermit crab that needs a home. Read and enjoy *Is This a House for Hermit Crab?*

4. Have the children tell you some of the house hunting problems the hermit crab encountered. How was the problem solved?

5. In the pocket chart place the repeated lines, *"So he stepped along the shore, by the sea, in the sand...scritch–scratch, scritch–scratch."* As you reread this story, track this phrase each time it occurs and have the children chant or read.

6. Using the book as a guide, help the children sequence the pictures of all the different houses that the hermit crab visited. Using phonetic clues, the children are now able to match the

words to the houses. Chant or read from the pocket chart.

7. Referring to the pocket chart, have the children describe the problem with the houses. As each one is mentioned, place the matching phrase on the appropriate line.

8. Distribute all the picture and word cards. The children will need to find their *partners* and rebuild the lesson in the pocket chart.

9. Help the children retell the story, using the pocket chart as a guide. Discuss what else the hermit crab might have considered using for his house.

10. Introduce *A House for Hermit Crab* by Eric Carle, telling the children that this hermit crab also had a house problem. Read and enjoy this delightful adventure. Compare and contrast the problems of the two hermit crabs.

11. Ask the children when this story took place. Through discussion we want to elicit from the children that this journey took a year to complete. Have the children chant the months of the year as you place those word cards in the pocket chart.

12. Referring back to the book, help the children recall what happened in each month. For example, in January he had no shell and went house hunting. Place that picture of the hermit crab with no shell (blackline 60) in the pocket chart next to the word *January*.

13. Reread the story to be certain that the sequencing was correct. As you come to the month of March, place in the pocket chart the sentence strip that has "_____*Hermit Crab picked it up with his claw and placed it on his shell.*" Have the children tell you how the sea anemone was picked up and discuss the meaning of the word *gently*. Each child dramatizes "gently picking up..." Place that word card on top of the blank space and read or chant. Continue in the same manner with the months April–July.

14. Group your children into partners and have them retell this story to each other. They may refer to the pocket chart as needed.

15. As an added treat, you may wish to dramatize this story using the hat and pictures (enlarged versions of blacklines 60–62) that you prepared earlier. The child who is Hermit Crab wears the hat and crawls on all fours. Other children take the parts of the sea anemone, starfish, coral, snails, sea urchin, seaweed, bright lantern fish, pebbles, little hermit crab and new shell. As Hermit Crab meets each of the first five characters, the actors attach their enlarged pictures to the hat. Those actors then move away. Hermit Crab continues his journey until he finds a new shell.

16. Brainstorm for possible decorations for his new shell.
    (This activity could go on and on and on...)

Extension: *Art*

1. Have the children finger paint on large finger paint paper – one color to a paper. An easy way to do this is to have five groups, having each group work with a different color. (Red, yellow, blue, green and grey.) Each child finger paints two pages of his/her color – thus, the group produces twelve pages of each color. Cut these into thirds and you will have a piece of each color for every child in your class.

2. Each child needs a copy of the empty shell and Hermit Crab (blacklines 63–64). Sponge paint Hermit Crab red. Refer to the cover of the book for ideas on sponge painting the shell. Cut out both pictures. Be sure to slit the shell on the dotted line so Hermit Crab is able to move in and out. On 12″ x 18″ light blue or white construction paper carefully glue down the outside edges of the shell, thus creating a "home" for Hermit Crab.

3. The children will now decorate Hermit Crab's shell using the prepared finger painted papers. Though this is a time consuming project, the results are more than worth the effort!

Activity 12

There's A Hole In The Bottom Of The Sea

Materials:

Materials needed:

- Blacklines 65–66 for the pocket chart
- 7 pieces of 5" x 6" tagboard cards for the pocket chart
- Blacklines 67–69 for the individual booklets
- 4" x 9" manila or white construction paper for the *hole* page and *seaweed* page of the booklet
- Sentence strips
- Felt pens
- Contact paper or laminating film

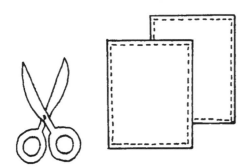

Preparation:

1. Color, cut and mount blacklines 65–66 on 5" x 6" tagboard cards. Contact or laminate.

2. Duplicate blacklines 67–68 for the booklet on 9" x 12" white or manila construction paper (one set per child). Note that there are no lines separating the three booklet pages that appear on each blackline. Cut so that each of the three pieces will measure 9" x 4".

3. For kindergarten duplicate blackline 69, one per four children, on any light colored paper. Cut in fourths. If you would like your first grade children to write these words, you will need to cut seven light colored strips of paper.

4. On sentence strips print the following:

	Guess who's
in the	There's a mirror
on the	There's a mermaid
on the	There's a sea chest
on the	There's a boat
in the	There's seaweed
in the	There's a hole
It is me	in the bottom of the sea

5. You will notice that there is no booklet blackline for the **hole page** or the **seaweed page**. We like to cut and paste a dark oval for the hole and use torn green tissue or construction paper for the seaweed. Crayons work fine also.

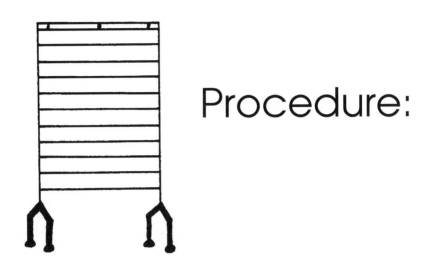

Procedure:

1. Introduce our version of the old camp song, ***There's A Hole In The Bottom Of The Sea***. This is a cumulative song in which a new phrase is added to each verse.

   There's a hole in the bottom of the sea,
   There's a hole in the bottom of the sea,
   There's a hole, there's a hole,
   There's a hole in the bottom of the sea.

   There's seaweed in the hole in the bottom of the sea,
   There's seaweed in the hole in the bottom of the sea,
   There's a hole, there's a hole,
   There's a hole in the bottom of the sea.

   There's a boat in the seaweed in the hole in the bottom of the sea.

There's a sea chest on the boat in the seaweed in the hole in the bottom of the sea.

There's a mermaid on the sea chest on the boat in the seaweed in the hole in the bottom of the sea.

There's a mirror on the mermaid on the sea chest on the boat in the seaweed in the hole in the bottom of the sea.

Guess who's in the mirror on the mermaid on the sea chest on the boat in the seaweed in the hole in the bottom of the sea.
It is me! It is me!
It is me in the bottom of the sea!

Place the appropriate **pictures** in the pocket chart as you sing. This song will be built from the bottom of the pocket chart to the top. It will also be necessary to leave the very bottom pocket empty as you will need it for the last line of each verse.

2. Sing several times until the children are able to join in with you.
3. Help the children match the phrases (There's a hole, There's seaweed, etc.) to the appropriate pictures in the pocket chart. Read.
4. Distribute the picture cards along with the phrases to the class. They will find their partners and rebuild the song in the pocket chart. At this time add the phrase *in the bottom of the sea* to the bottom pocket. Read.

Note: Because this song is quite lengthy, we didn't suggest that you print the entire text of every stanza on sentence strips. Simply track the repeated phrases as needed.

5. This is a good time to discuss the contractions *there's* and *who's*. Depending on your grade level, you may have to present a lesson on what makes up a contraction.

6. For ease in this next step you will want to stack the remaining word cards in this order:

> in the
> on the
> on the
> on the
> in the
> in the
> *It is me!*

7. To complete the song, add the remaining word cards *(in the, on the, etc.)* as you sing each verse. Place these words **directly on top of** the words *there's a* to create the new phrase. See the following illustration.

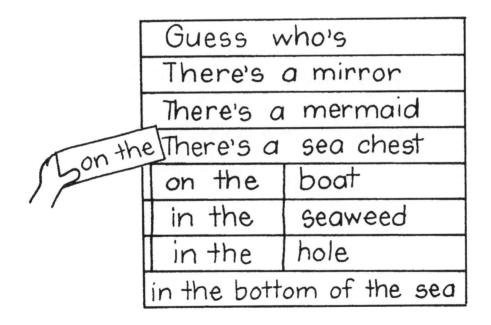

For the last stanza, place the words *It is me!* in front of the phrase, *in the bottom of the sea.* If this is the first time you have used this song, you might want to practice using the cards in the pocket chart before using it in the classroom.

Extension: *Individual Booklet*

1. The children will color the pictures from blacklines 67–68. They may use the side of a peeled blue crayon to create the effect of water.

2. For the hole page, cut and glue down a dark oval. Add sand at the bottom. For the seaweed page, use either torn green tissue, torn construction paper or simply illustrate with crayons.

3. Distribute the words from blackline 69 (or blank strips if your children will write their own words) and have the children match the words to the pictures. Glue to the bottom of each page.

4. For a reflection effect glue either mylar or foil to the inside area of the mirror.

5. For the last page, children may either draw themselves in the mirror or you may wish to attach a small school picture.

6. The children are now able to sequence the book and staple. Sing together, using the booklet as a guide.

Activity 13 — *The Twelve Days of Summer*

Materials:

Materials needed:

- *The Twelve Days of Summer* by Elizabeth O'Donnell
- Small 6″ colored paper plates (two per child)
- Sentence strips
- Colored felt pens
- 12″ x 18″ light blue construction paper
- Laminating film or contact paper
- A package of inexpensive pearl–like beads (one bead per child)
- Pastel tissue paper if you make an oyster
- Blacklines 70–74 for the *Twelve Days* pocket chart activity
- Blackline 75 for *Oyster in the Deep* chart
- Rubberband for strip book
- For blacklines 70-74 you will need the following sizes of tagboard:
  — 12 pieces of 5″ x 6″ tagboard cards
  — 12 pieces of 3″ x 3″ tagboard cards
  — 12 pieces of 2½″ x 4½″ tagboard cards

Preparation:

1. Color, cut and mount blacklines 70–72 on 5″ x 6″ tagboard cards. Contact or laminate.
2. Cut and mount blacklines 73–74 on 2½″ x 4½″ and 3″ x 3″ tagboard cards. Contact or laminate.
3. On sentence strips print the phrases from the book, *The Twelve Days of Summer.* (A little purple sea anemone, two pelicans, etc.)
4. Color, cut and laminate or contact blackline 75 for the chart paper song.
5. Print the following song, *Oyster in the Deep,* on chart paper:

Oyster in the Deep

Oyster in the deep,
Oyster in the deep,
She had a pearl she wanted to keep
Oyster in the deep.

Along came a clam,
Along came a clam,
He took the pearl, said, "Thank-you ma'am!"
Along came a clam.

Along came a crab,
Along came a crab,
He took the pearl with a giant grab,
Along came a crab.

Along came a snail,
Along came a snail,
He took the pearl, hid it in his pail,
Along came a snail.

The snail went to sleep,
The snail went to sleep,
The pearl just wasn't his to keep,
The snail went to sleep.

The oyster in the deep,
The oyster in the deep,
She found a pearl that she could keep,
The oyster in the deep.

6. Next to each stanza, glue the appropriate pictures from blackline 75.

7. Prepare the strip book. Fold six to eight sentence strips. Bind in the middle with a rubberband. (This will give you twelve to eighteen pages.) On the front write *"Oysters..."*.

8. You may need to do a bit of research on oysters. If you do not have a reference book available, here are some basic facts. Oysters:

- are mollusks
- have two shells, held firmly together by a strong muscle
- have hard shells
- feed on tiny plants and animals in the water
- live on the ocean bottom
- are man's most valuable shellfish because they produce pearls
- live about six years

- are used for food
- are filter feeders
- produce pearls from a grain of sand or some other object that gets inside the shell and rubs against the oyster's body
- that produce pearls live in the Pacific Ocean or the Persian Gulf for the most part

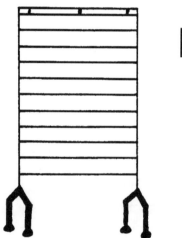

Procedure:

1. Introduce this activity with the whimsical song, *Oyster in the Deep* which is sung to the tune of *Farmer in the Dell.* Track on the chart as you sing.

2. This song will be memorized with just a few repetitions. The class is now able to dramatize this song with all the children taking all the parts.

3. Show the children a pearl and ask them to tell you everything they know about pearls. Read any factual books you have on oysters. Discuss this information and review what the children initially came up with. Are there any facts that need to be altered or revised?

4. Now record one fact on each page of the prepared strip book.

Have the class read this *instant book* and add it to your class library.

5. Sing and enjoy the book, *The Twelve Days of Summer.* Ask the children if this song reminds them of another old favorite. Compare and contrast the two songs. Sing again, with the children joining in during the countdown.

6. Place all the ordinal numeral cards in the pocket chart. Chant with the class, "1st day, 2nd day, 3rd day, etc.."

7. Distribute the cardinal numeral cards to the children. Have the children sequence these cards in the pocket chart along side the ordinal numerals.

8. Now distribute the picture cards to the class. Have the children add these to the pocket chart in the correct sequence.
   Chant or sing from the pocket chart.

9. Distribute all picture and numeral cards to the children and have the class rebuild. Sing to check for accuracy.

1st day	A	🎆	
2nd day	2	🦆	
3rd day	3	🪼	
4th day	4		
5th day	5		

10. To prepare for a rewrite, ask the children if they can think of any other sea creatures they might see on a summer day. Record the brainstorming on the chalkboard.

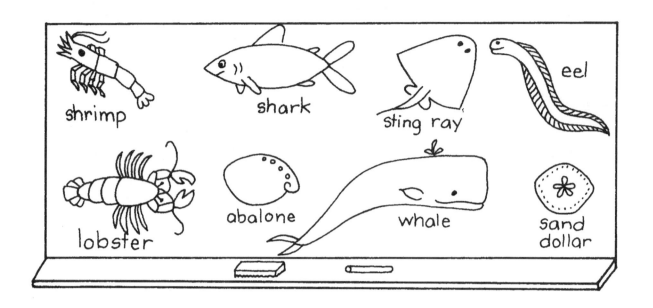

 Extension: *Our 12 Days of Summer class book and Paper Plate Art*

Class Book: The class as a whole needs to decide which twelve items to use in the rewrite. A cardinal number is assigned to each of those items. Now, chanting as you go, help the children choose additional words to maintain the meter of the song. (6 pinching lobsters, 5 mean old sharks, 4 humungus whales, 3 icky eels, 2 little shrimp and a teeny tiny abalone.)

Divide up the number of sea creatures (there are seventy-eight!) so that each child has two or three to create. We like to have the children use tempra and paint the items. We then add felt pen fea-

98

tures or outlines, cut the pictures out and glue them to the 12"x 18" construction paper pages of the book. You will need to print the text for each page and add a cover. Laminate or contact and bind together. Sing several times.

Note: If you have did not make one of the other bulletin boards, or have enormous wall space, you may wish to create a bulletin board and use the title, *Our 12 Days of Summer.* Simply use brown and blue butcher paper. The children would prepare the seventy-eight sea creatures (as described in the rewrite) and then add them to the bulletin board. Write the words on sentence strips and place these next to each item.

Paper Plate Art – *Oyster*: you will need pink plates. If you do not have pink ones, simply paint two 6" white plates, both inside and out. For the inside, wad up plain newsprint into a 4" x 1" x 6" oval. Cover this with pink tissue paper (or you may wish to only use tissue paper.) Glue the tissue paper oval to the inside of one plate. Put a few drops of glue on the inside of the other plate. Carefully, fit the second plate over the first and staple the plates together on one side, along the rim. Leave one side open. Cut eyes out of construction paper and glue the eyes on the tissue paper. Add a pearl bead.

Fish: If you are using white plates, paint (any color) the outside and the inner rims of two paper plates. Cut tail and fins from a different color of construction paper. Outline the tail and fins with a black felt tip marker. Add any other features you wish, such as spots, dots or lines. Glue the tail and the fins to the inside rim of one of the plates. Staple the two plates together along the inside rim. Cut out eyes and any other features you choose and glue to the paper plates.

Optional Activities

Down In The Deep Alphabet Book – Two books that we like are both by Jerry Pallotta. *The Underwater Alphabet Book* deals with the most colorful creatures living on the coral reef. *The Ocean Alphabet Book* contains fish and other creatures that live in the North Atlantic Ocean. At the end of this theme the children have enormous knowledge about the sea and it is fairly easy to help the class think of a sea creature for each letter of the alphabet. Each child then takes one letter and illustrates for a class book.

Baby Beluga – This is a delightful *Song to Read* book by Raffi, which is also available on record or tape. It is a favorite with children and a great springboard for exploring whale facts. First graders are able to do some simple factual writing after learning about the different kinds of whales and their habits.

Swimmy – This ageless tale by Leo Lionni has been a classroom treasure for years. The message of friendship, courage and problem solving are developed in a beautiful format. An art project that illustrates the wonderful ending of this story is easily accomplished by using a small fish cut-out and crayons. Each child draws his/her own cut-out on light weight tagboard. This is cut out and placed under a 12″ x 18″ piece of construction paper. Using the side of a peeled crayon, the children rub gently over the cut-out which creates one fish. Continue in this manner, moving the cut-out to create an entire school of fish. Be sure to place Swimmy as the eye of the *big fish.*

Note: This was an art idea we got from Wyn Davies of Canada. Children may wish to create other groups of sea creatures using cut-outs. Refer to the book *Fishes* by Brian Wildsmith for some excellent ideas.

The Magic Fish – This enriching folktale, adapted by Freya Littledale, is an excellent book to help develop the concept of quotation marks. Print on sentence strips several quotations from the story. Also print *said the fisherman*, *said the fish* and *said the wife*. Place these three phrases in the pocket chart. Display one quotation at a time, having the children recall which character said it, and place that quotation in the proper place.

Dramatization is also a must for this story.

I Like Fish – This poem is found in *The Friendly Book* by Margaret Wise Brown. The book seems to come in and go out of print quite often. Please check your library if you cannot find a copy in your local bookstore. This is a rewrite of her *I Like Bugs* poem. It is easily developed in the pocket chart because of the repetition and simple format. After developing this poem orally, brainstorm for other kinds of fish and where they might be found. Children are then able to complete a rewrite, either individually or as a group.

Blue Sea – This is a book of few words by Donald Crews. It can be developed in the pocket chart and chanted. A natural extension for this tale would be to sort sea creatures by little, big, bigger and biggest.

Grandpa, Grandpa – This is a big book by Joy Cowley, distributed by The Wright Group. This book is easily memorized by small children and the format makes a rewrite simple.

Cooking – Brainstorming for ingredients in clam chowder is fun. Have a tasting party including items the children might not be familiar with – squid, seaweed, clam chowder, oyster stew, halibut, crab, lobster, tuna, shrimp, scallops, etc.

Bibliography

Allen, Pamela, *Who Sank The Boat?*, Coward-McCann, Inc., New York, NY, 1982.

Althea, *Undersea Homes*, Cambridge University Press, New York, NY, 1985.

Banks, Margaret, *One, One, The Beach Is Fun*, offered by The Big Book Bin Inc., P.O. Box 800-480, Abbotsford, B.C., V2S 6H1, Canada.

Baratta-Lorton, Mary, *Mathematics Their Way*, Addison-Wesley Publishing Company, Reading, MA, 1976.

Barton, Byron, *Boats*, Thomas Y. Crowell, New York, NY, 1986.

Beharrell, Gayle (Illustrator), *I Took A Trip Down To The Sea*, The Big Book Bin Inc., P.O. Box 8000-480, Abbotsford, B.C., V2S 6H1 Canada.

Brown, Margaret Wise, *The Friendly Book*, Golden Press, Western Publishing Group, Inc., New York, NY, 1954.

Burningham, John, *Come Away From The Water, Shirley*, A Harper Trophy Book, Thomas Y. Crowell, New York, NY, 1977.

Burningham, John, *Mr Gumpy's Outing*, Henry Holt and Company, New York, NY, 1970.

Carle, Eric, *A House for Hermit Crab*, Picture Book Studio, Saxonville, MA, 1987.

Clements, Andrew, *Big Al*, Picture Book Studio, Saxonville, MA., 1988.

Cole, Sheila, *When the Tide is Low*, Lothrop, Lee & Shepard Books, New York, NY, 1985.

Crampton, Gertrude, *Scuffy The Tugboat*, Golden Press, Western Publishing Group, Inc., New York, NY, 1955.

Crenson, Victoria, *Sea Creatures*, Price, Stern Sloan, Inc., Los Angeles, CA, 1988.

Crews, Donald, *Harbor*, Mulberry Books, New York, NY, 1982.

Diamond, Charlotte, *Octopus,* distributed by The Big Book Bin Inc., P.O. Box 800-480, Abbotsford, B.C. V2S 6H1, Canada.

Dijs, Carla, *Who Sees You? At The Ocean,* Grosset & Dunlap, New York, NY, 1987.

Domanska, Janina, *If All The Seas Were One Sea,* Macmillan Publishing Company, New York, NY, 1971.

Eastman, David, *What is a Fish,* Troll Associates, Mahwah, NJ, 1982.

Edwards, Roberta, *Five Silly Fishermen,* Random House, New York, NY, 1989.

Ehlert, Lois, *Fish Eyes; A Book You Can Count On,* Harcourt Brace Jovanovich, Publishers, New York, NY, 1990.

Elkin, Benjamin, *Six Foolish Fishermen,* Scholastic Inc., New York, NY, 1957.

Emberley, Ed, *Ed Emberley's Drawing Book of Animals,* Little, Brown and Company, Boston, MA, 1970.

Emberley, Ed, *Ed Emgerley's Great Thumbprint Drawing Book,* Little, Brown and Company, Boston, MA, 1977.

Emberley, Ed, *Ed Emberley's Picture Pie,* Little, Brown and Company, Boston, MA, 1984.

Florian, Douglas, *Discovering Seashells,* Charles Scribner's Sons, New York, NY, 1986.

Fowler, Richard, *Mr. Little's Noisy Boat,* Grosset & Dunlap, New York, NY, 1986.

Ginsburg, Mirra, *Four Brave Sailors,* Greenwillow Books, New York, NY, 1987.

Gomi, Taro, *Where's the Fish?,* William Morrow and Company, Inc., New York, NY, 1977.

Heller, Ruth, *How to Hide An Octopus & Other Sea Creatures,* Grosset & Dunlap, New York, NY, 1985.

Hoy, Key, *Nature Pop-Ups Water Life,* Ideals Children's Books, Nashville, TN, 1990.

Hulme, Joy N., *Sea Squares,* Hyperion Books for Children, USA, 1991.

Jablonsky, Alice, *Discover Ocean Life*, Publications International, Ltd., IL, 1991.

Kalan, Robert, *Blue Sea*, Greenwillow Books, New York, NY, 1979.

Kraus, Robert, *Herman the Helper*, Prentice-Hall Books for Young Readers, New York, NY, 1974.

Kunhardt, Edith, *Giant Sea Creatures*, A Golden Book, Western Publishing Group, Inc., New York, NY, 1984.

Lionni, Leo, *Swimmy*, Pinwheel Books, Toronto, Canada 1973.

Litchfield, Ada B., *It's Going To Rain!*, Atheneum, New York, NY, 1980.

Littledale, Freya, *The Magic Fish*, Scholastic, Inc., New York, NY, 1985.

MacCarthy, Patricia, *Ocean Parade — A Counting Book*, Dial Books for Young Readers, New York, NY, 1990.

Malnig, Anita, *Where the Waves Break — Life at the Edge of the Sea*, Carolrhoda Books, Inc., Minneapolis, MN, 1985.

McCloskey, Robert, *One Morning in Maine*, Picture Puffin, New York, NY, 1976.

McDonald, Megan, *Is This a House for Hermit Crab?*, Orchard Books, New York, NY, 1990.

McGowen, Tom, *Album of Whales*, Checkerboard Press, Macmillan, Inc., New York, NY, 1987.

Miller, Susanne Santoro, *Whales and Sharks and Other Creatures of the Deep*, Little Simon, New York, NY, 1982.

Morse, Doug, *The Sea Book*, Storyfold, Inc. MA, 1974.

O'Donnell, Elizabeth, *The Twelve Days Of Summer*, Morrow Junior Books, New York, NY, 1991.

Oppenheim, Joanne, *Follow That Fish*, A Bantam LIttle Rooster Book, Bank Street Ready To Read Series, A Byron Preiss Book, New York, NY, 1990.

Pallotta, Jetty, *The Ocean Alphabet Book*, Charlesbridge Publishing, MA, 1986.

Pallotta, Jerry, *The Underwater Alphabet Book*, Charlesbridge Publishing, MA, 1991.

Palmer, Helen, *A Fish Out Of Water*, Random House, Inc., New York, NY, 1961.

Podendorf, Illa, *A New True Book – Animals Of Sea And Shore,* Childrens Press, Chicago, IL, 1982.

Peet, Bill, *Kermit The Hermit,* Houghton Mifflin Company, Boston, MA, 1965.

Raffi and Wolff, Ashley, *Baby Beluga,* Crown Publishers, Inc., Raffi Songs to Read, New York, NY, 1990.

Raffi and Westcott, Nadine Bernard, *Raffi Songs to Read,* Crown Publishers, Inc., New York, NY, 1987.

Roop, Connie, *Keep the Lights Burning, Abbie,* Carolrhoda Books, Minneapolis, Minnesota, MN, 1985.

Roux, Charles and Plantain, Paul-Henry, *Ocean Dwellers,* Silver Burdett, Morristown, NJ, 1982.

Samtpm. Sheila White, *Beside the Bay,* Philomel Books, New York, NY, 1987.

Seymour, Peter, *What's at the Beach?,* Holt, Rinehart and Winston, New York, NY, 1985.

Seymour, Peter, *What's In The Deep Blue Sea?,* Henry Holt and Company, New York, NY, 1990.

Steig, William, *Amos & Boris,* Puffin Books, New York, NY, 1977.

Swift, Hildegarde H. and Ward, Lynd, *The Little Red Lighthouse And The Great Gray Bridge,* Harcourt Brace Jovanovich, Publishers, New York, NY, 1970.

Tokuda, Wendy and Hall, Richard, *Humphrey The Lost Whale,* Heian International, Inc., Union City, CA, 1986.

Wheeler, Alwyne, *Usborne First Nature – Fishes,* Usborne Publishing Ltd., London, England, 1982. Also by EDC Publishing, Tulsa, OK.

Wildsmith, Brian, *Fishes,* Oxford University Press, London, England, 1985.

Wylie, David & Joanne, *A Fishy Shape Story,* Childrens Press, Chicago, IL, 1984.

Wylie, David & Joanne, *A Funny Fish Story,* Childrens Press, Chicago, IL, 1984.

Wylie, David & Joanne, *A Fishy Color Story,* Childrens Press, Chicago, IL, 1983.

Blacklines

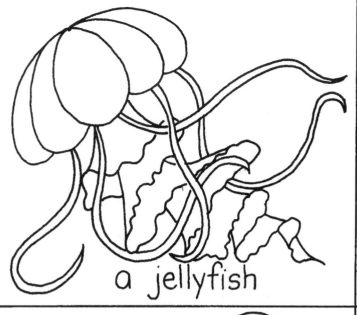

a jellyfish

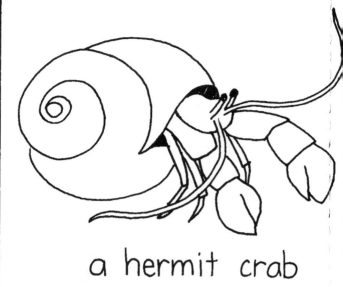

a hermit crab

an octopus

a seahorse

a shrimp

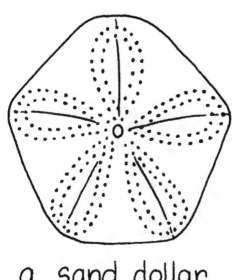

a sand dollar

a giant kelp fish

a whale

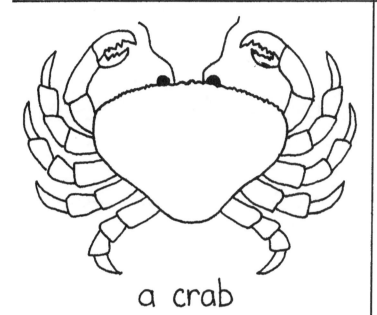

a crab

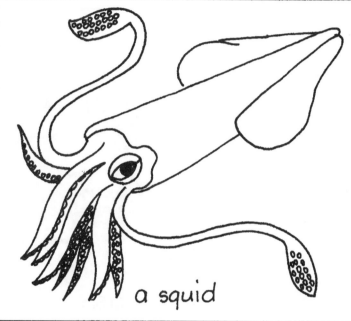

a squid

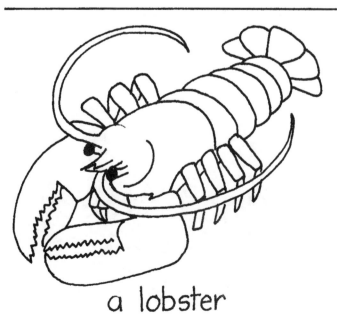

a lobster

a sea snail

a sea turtle

a great white shark

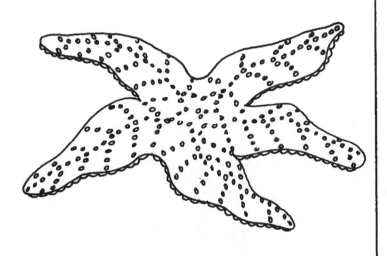

a starfish

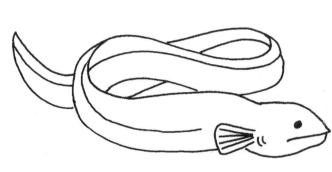

an eel

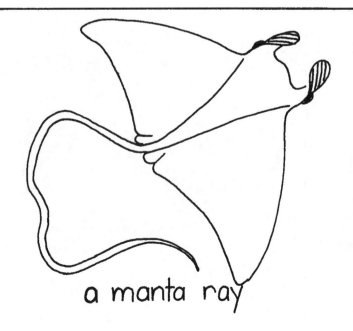

a manta ray

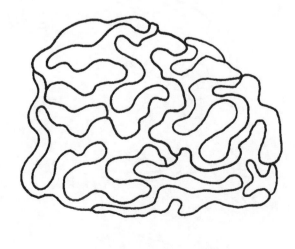

a sponge

a dolphin

a swordfish

a seagull

a seal

a sea otter

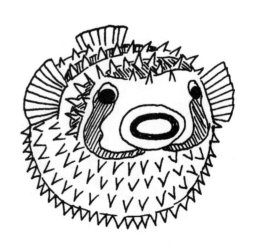

a porcupine fish

4

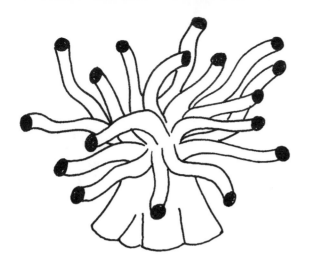

a sea anemone

a salmon

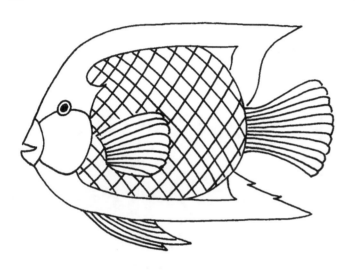

an angel fish

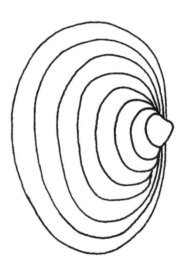

a clam

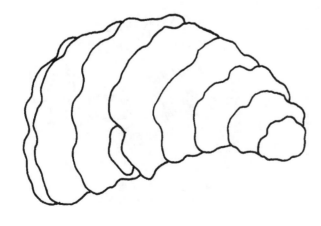

an oyster

a walrus

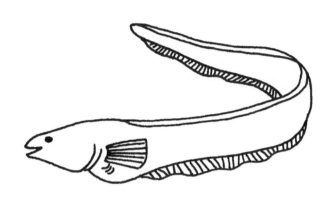

I took a trip
down to the sea.
What do you s'pose I saw?
I saw _____
and it _____
La, la, la, la, la, la.

11

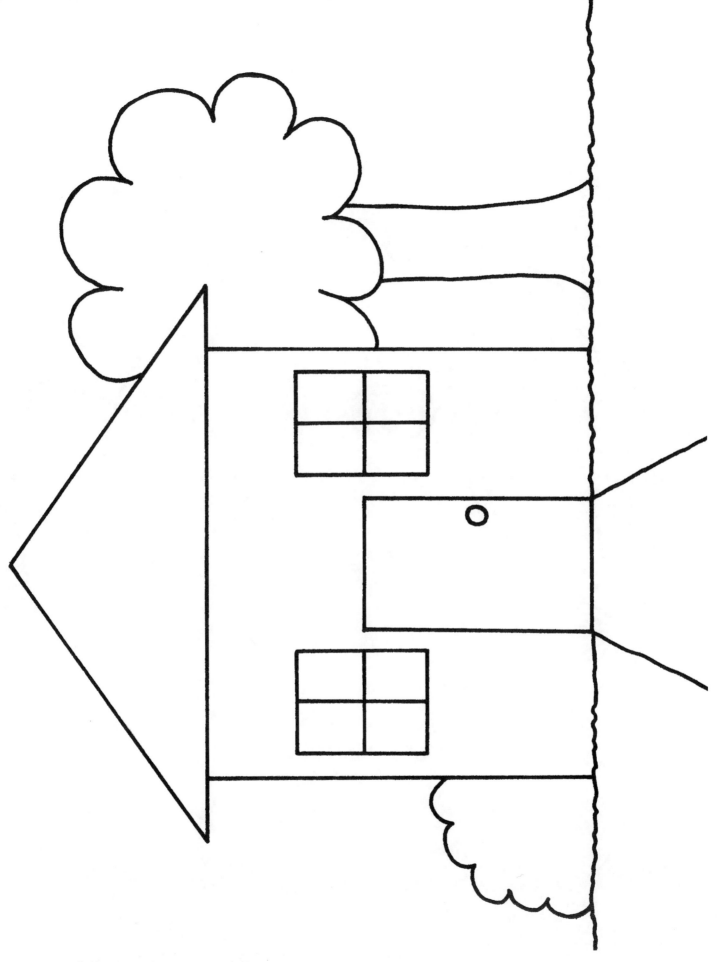

14

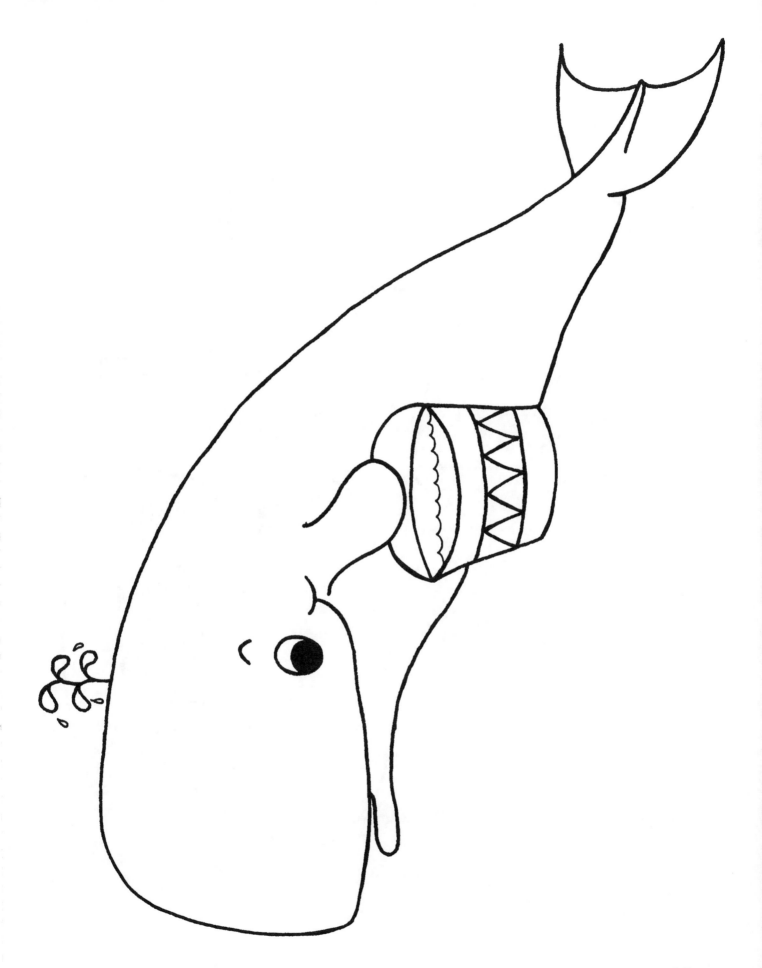

16

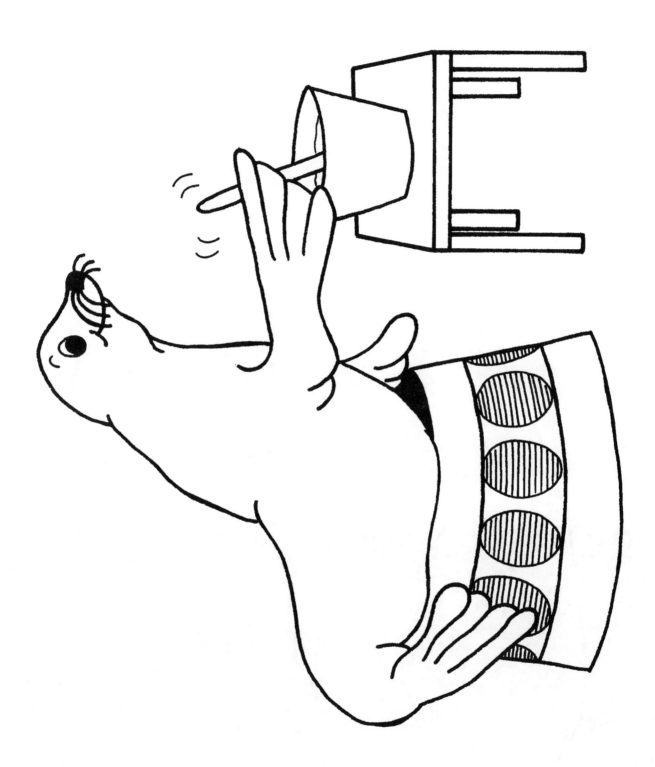

17

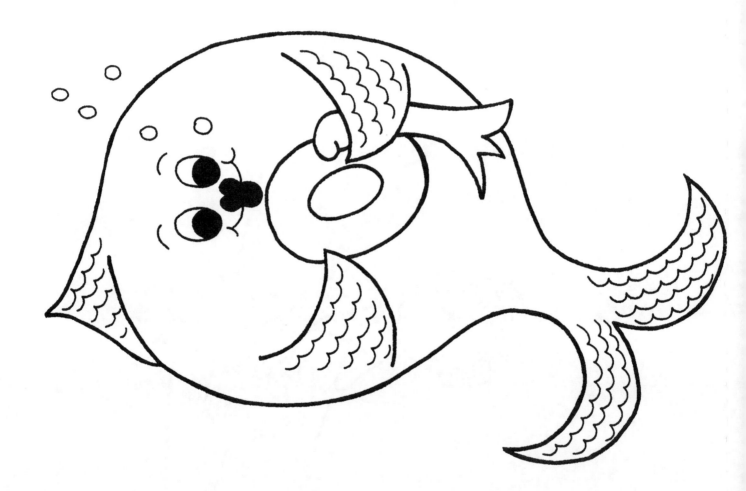

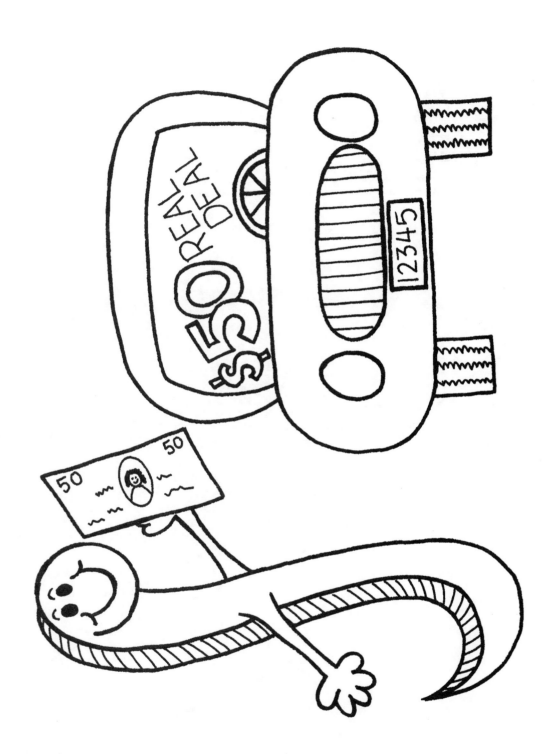

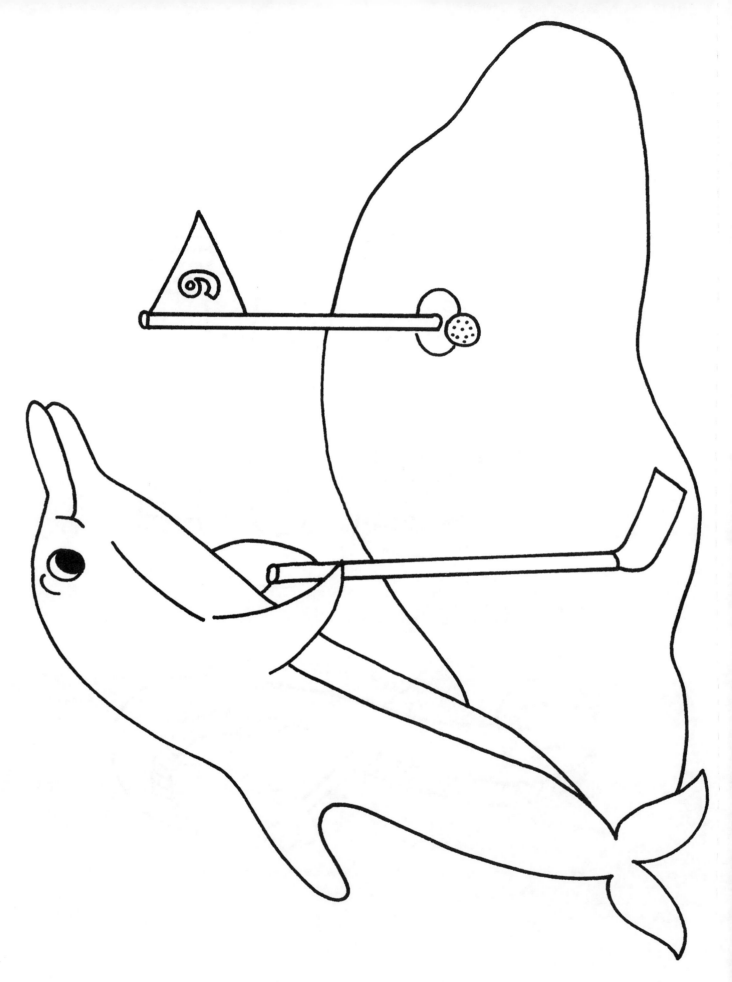

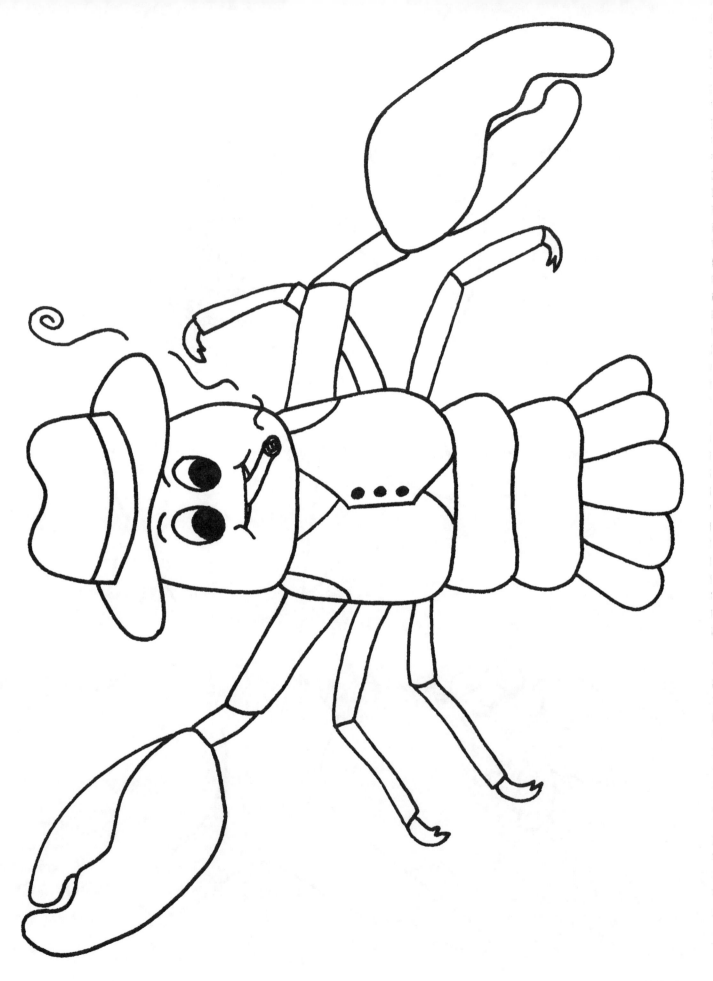

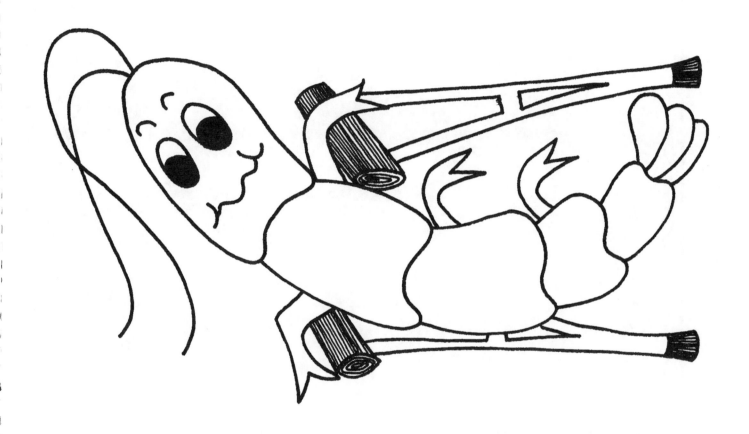

Did you ever see

Down in the deep?

Down by the blue sea
What can it be?
A little fish, a little fish
That's what I see.

Down by the blue sea
What can it be?
A big whale, a big whale
That's what I see.

Down by the blue sea
What can it be?
A starfish, a starfish
That's what I see.

Down by the blue sea
What can it be?
A seahorse, a seahorse
That's what I see.

Down by the blue sea
What can it be?
A black seal, a black seal
That's what I see.

Down by the blue sea
What can it be?
A seashell, a seashell
That's what I see.

Down by the blue sea
What can it be?
A sailboat, a sailboat
That's what I see.

Down by the blue sea
What can it be?
A sandy beach, a sandy beach
That's what I see.

Down by the blue sea
What can it be?
Me in a bathing suit
That's what I see.

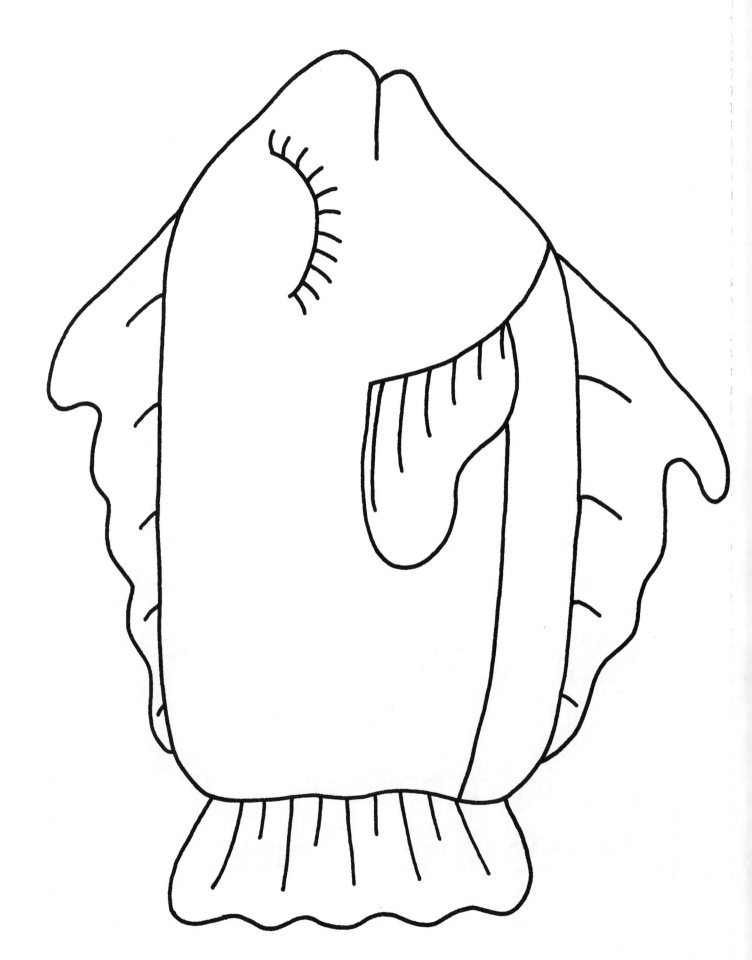

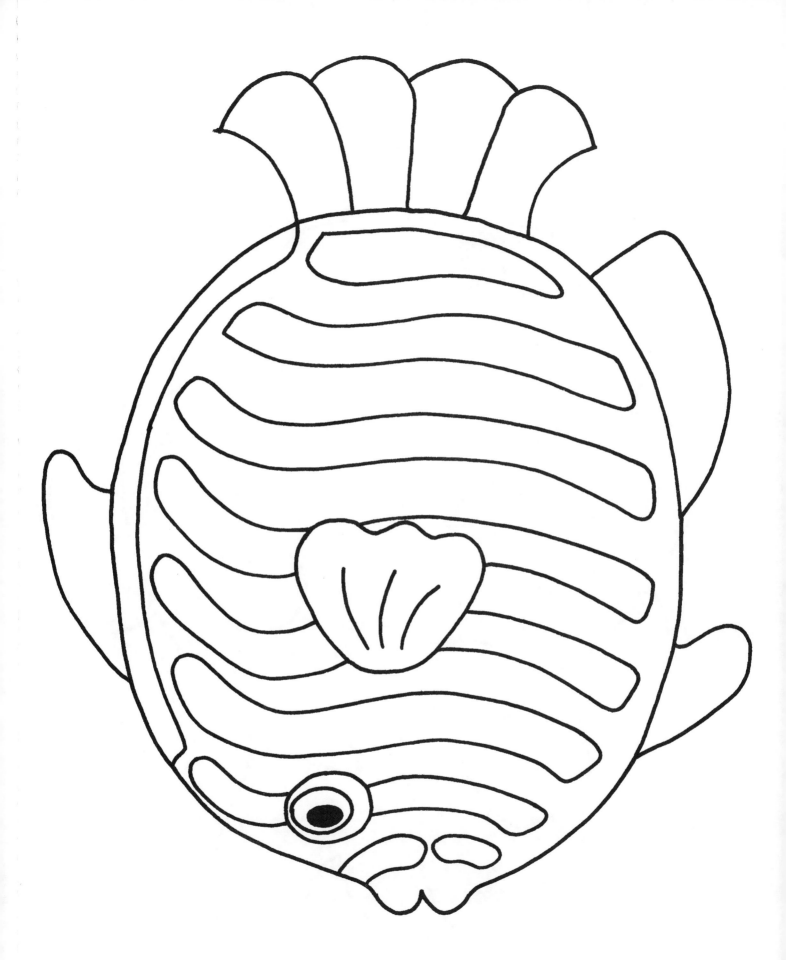

37

Fishy
Facts

by _____

Fishy
Facts

by _____

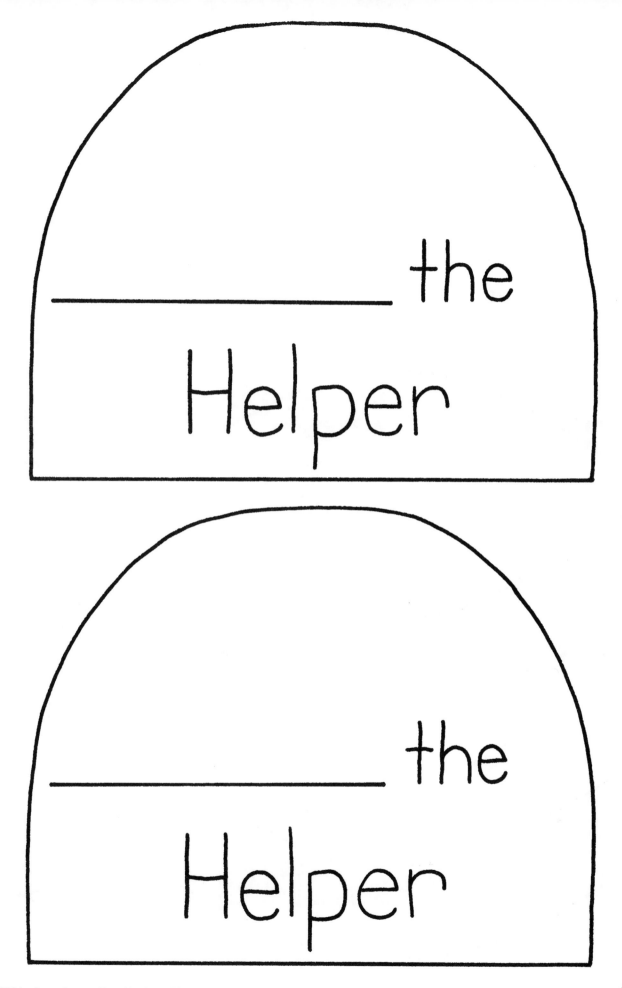

_____ the
Helper

_____ the
Helper

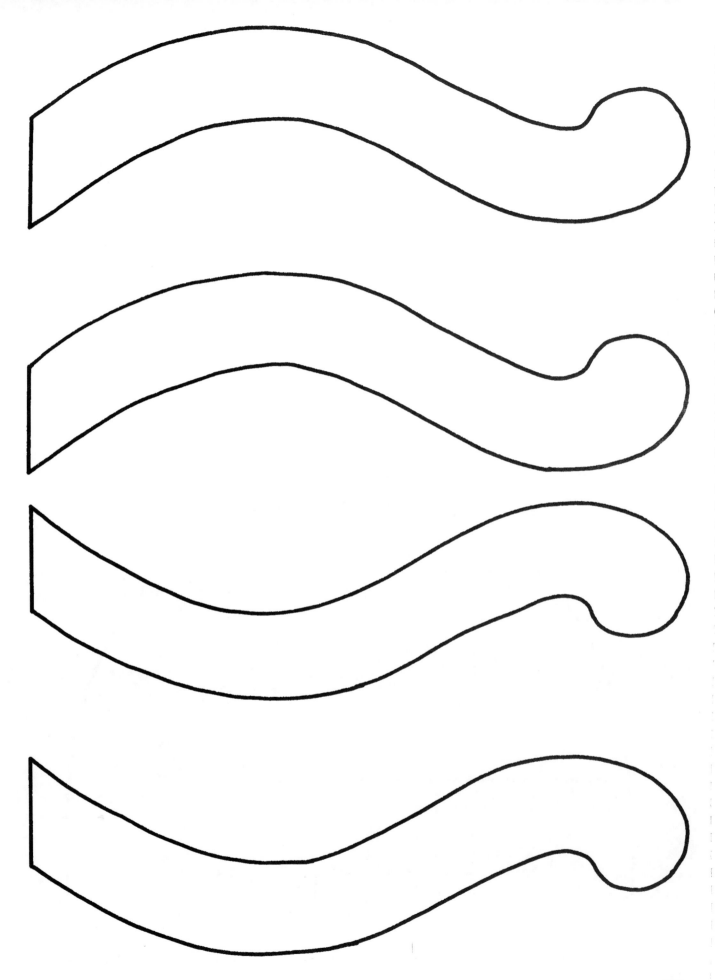

43

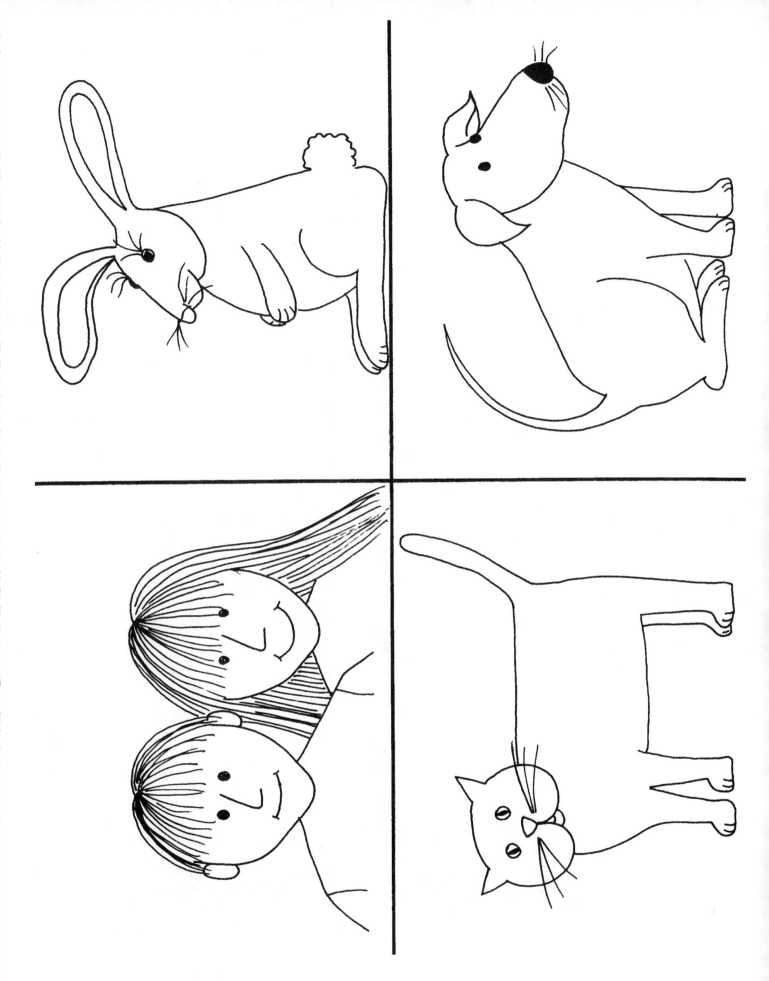

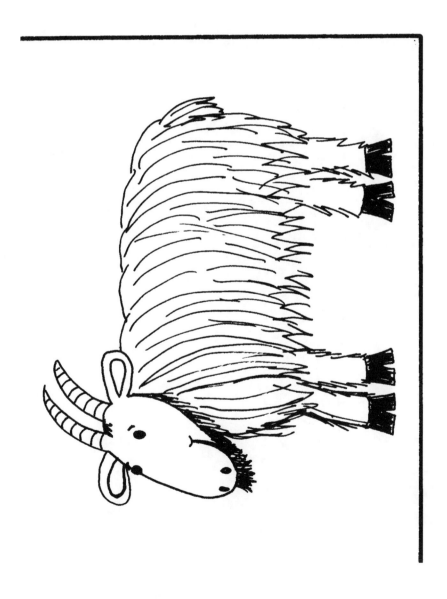

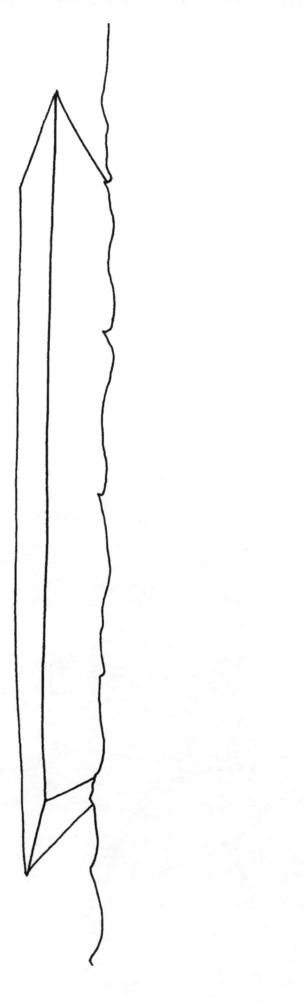

boat

_____

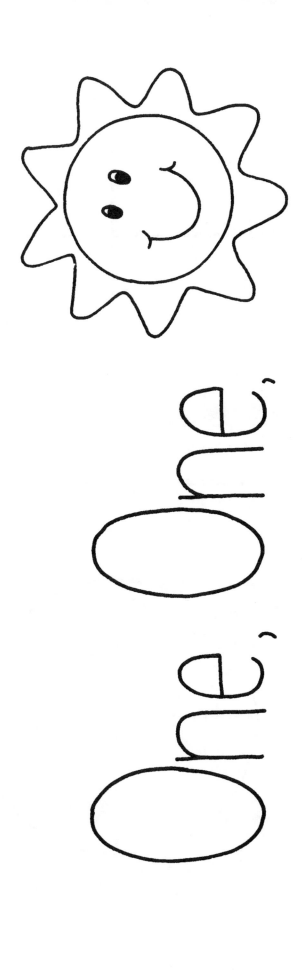

One, One,

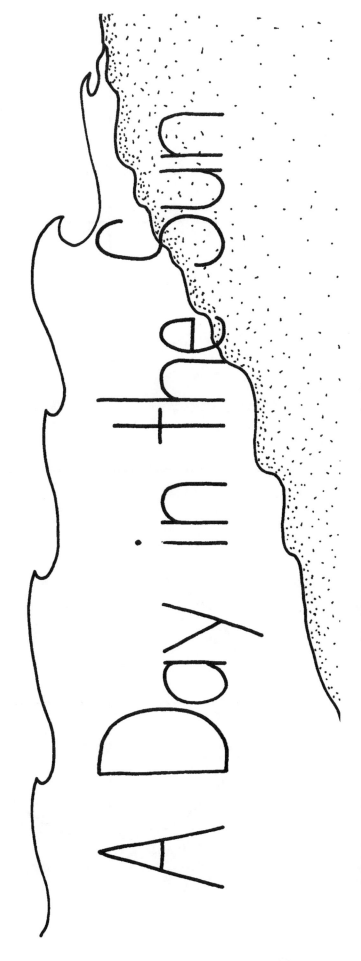

A Day in the Sun

48

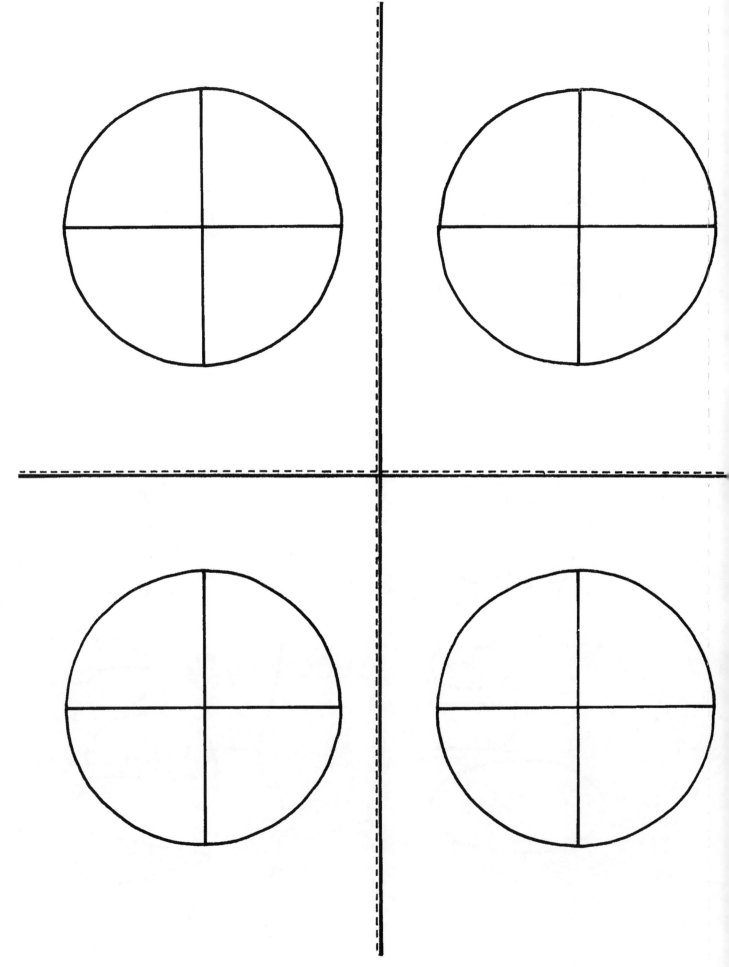

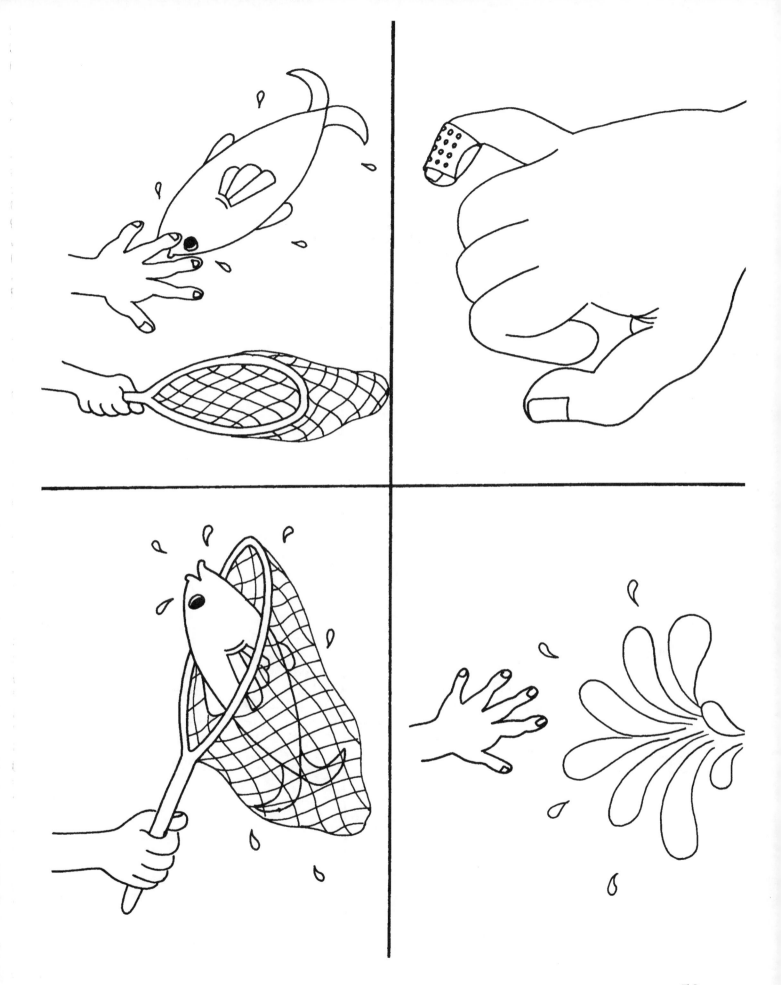

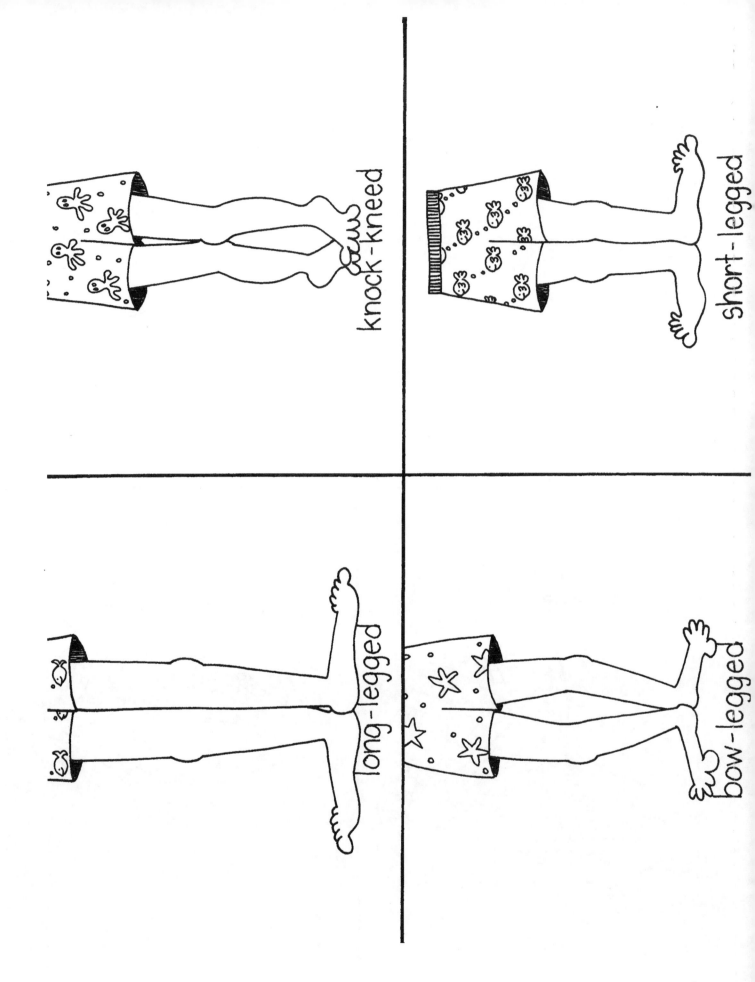

bald-headed

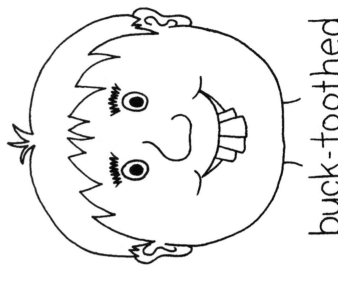

buck-toothed

cross - eyed

big-earred

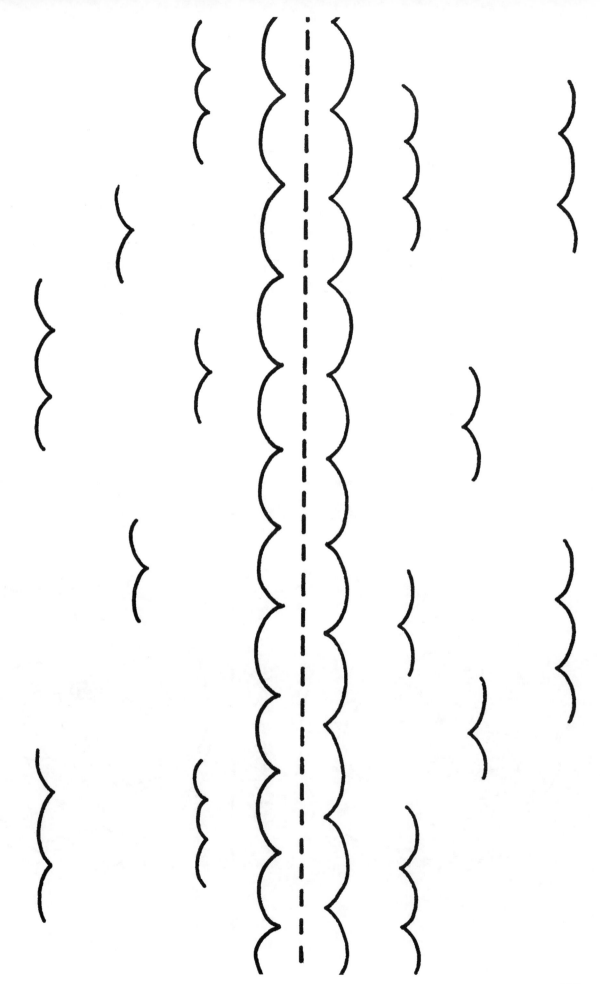

54

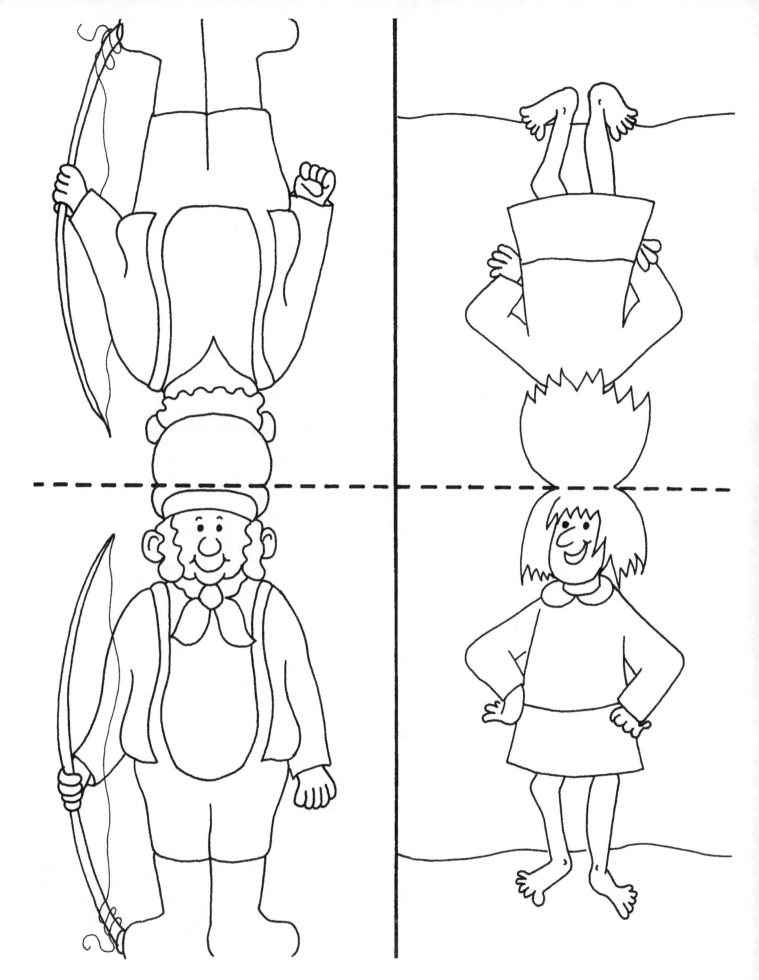

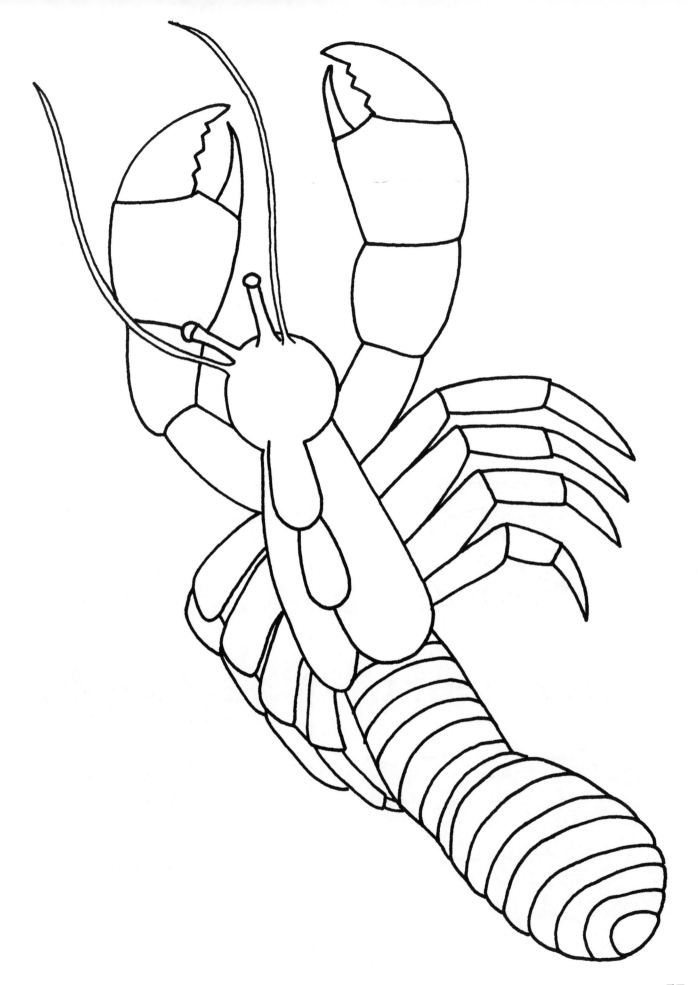

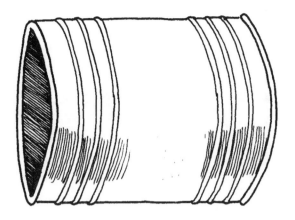

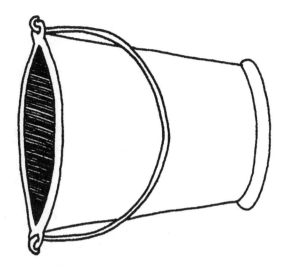

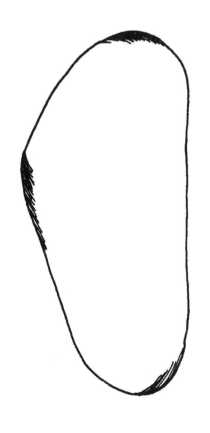

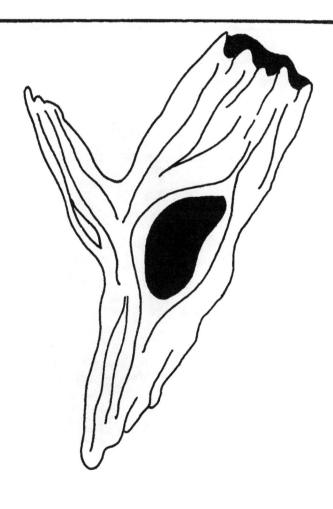

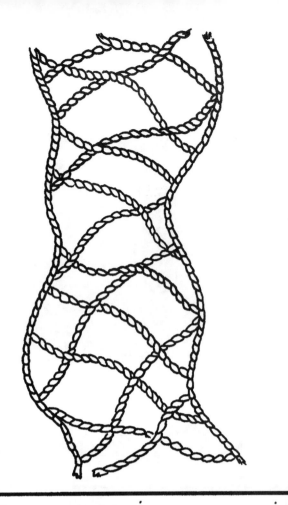

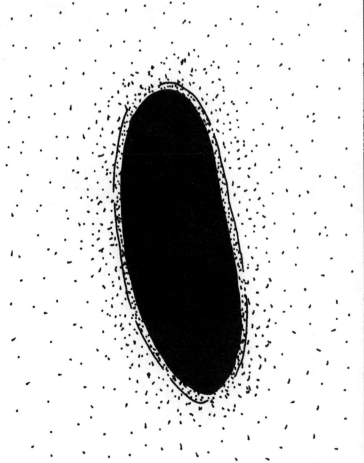

60

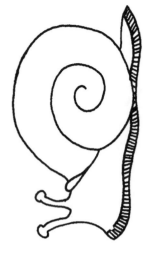

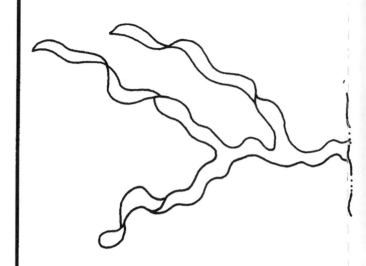

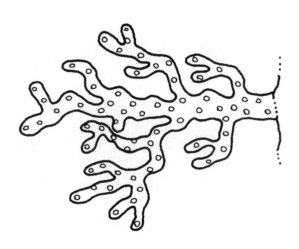

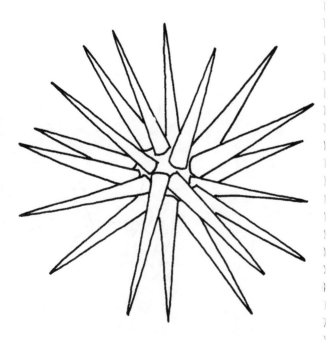

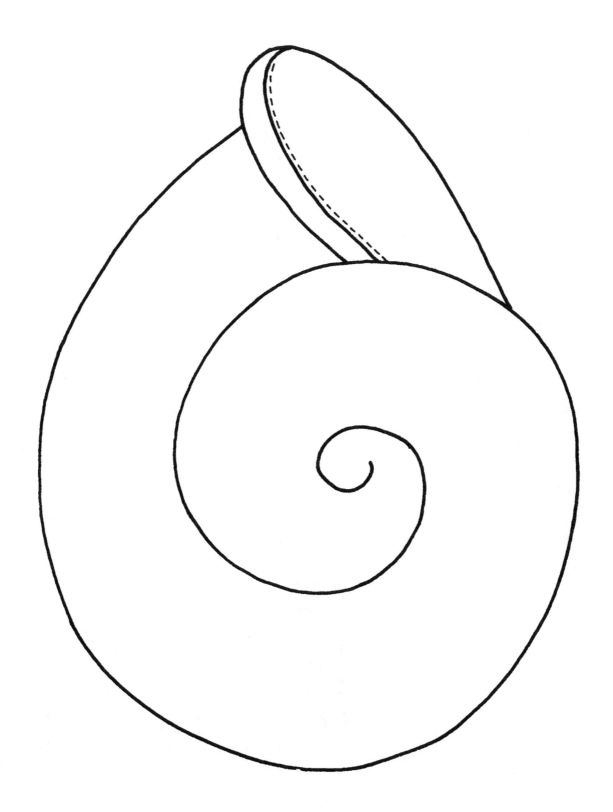

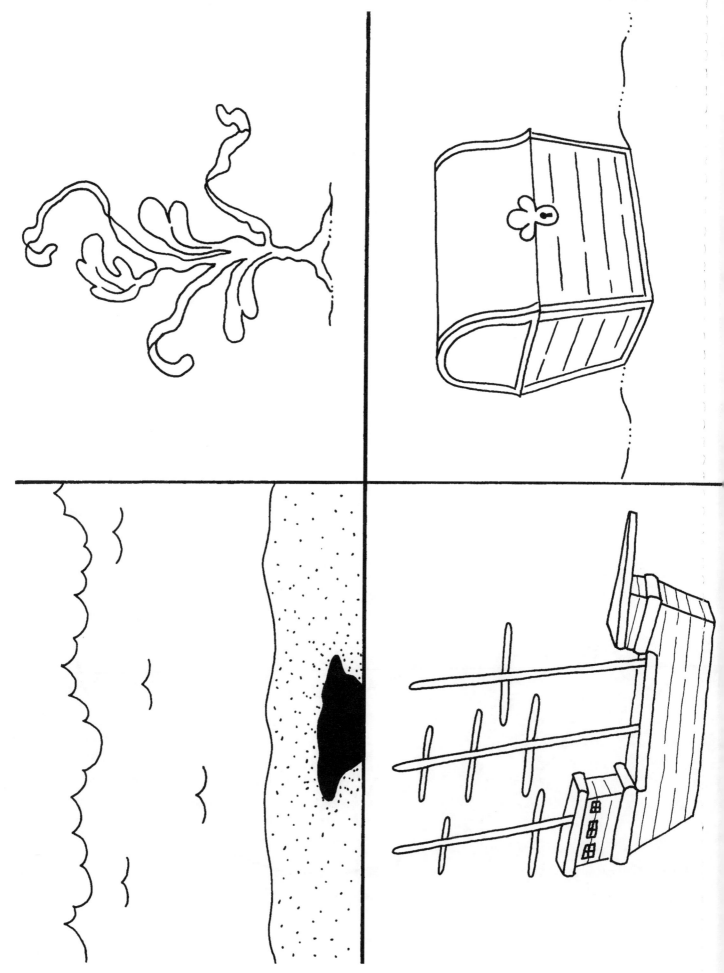

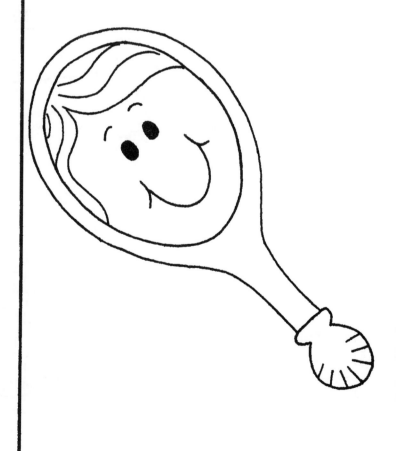

There's a hole
in the bottom
of the sea...

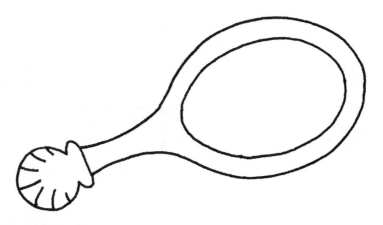

hole	hole
seaweed	seaweed
boat	boat
sea chest	sea chest
mermaid	mermaid
mirror	mirror
me	me
hole	hole
seaweed	seaweed
boat	boat
sea chest	sea chest
mermaid	mermaid
mirror	mirror
me	me

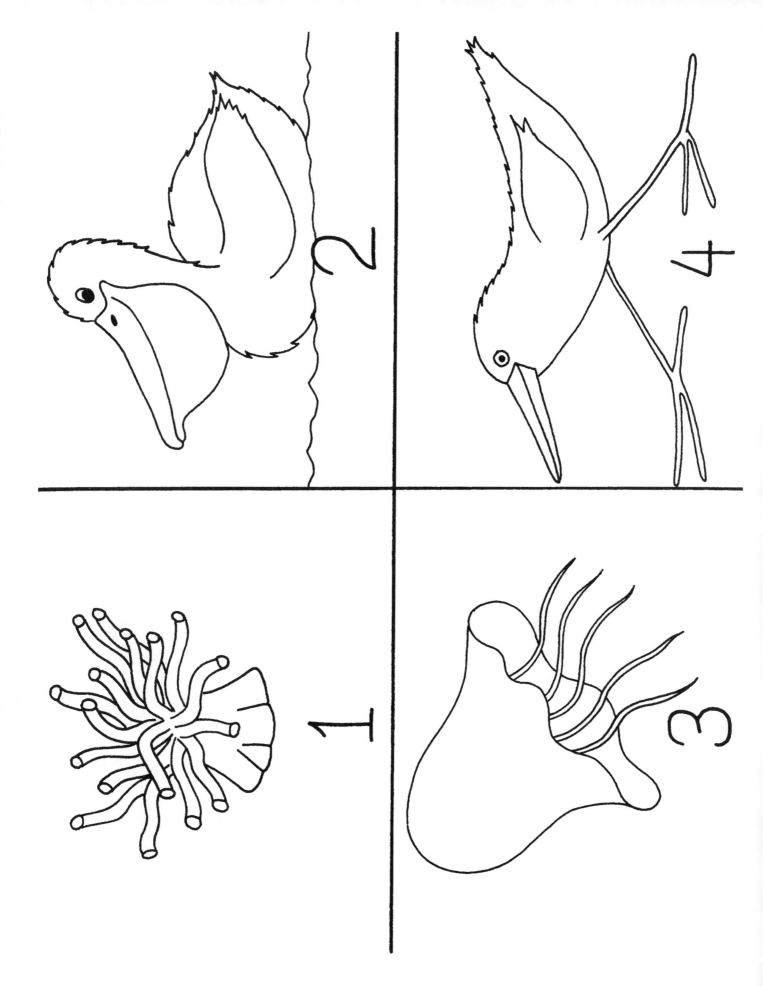

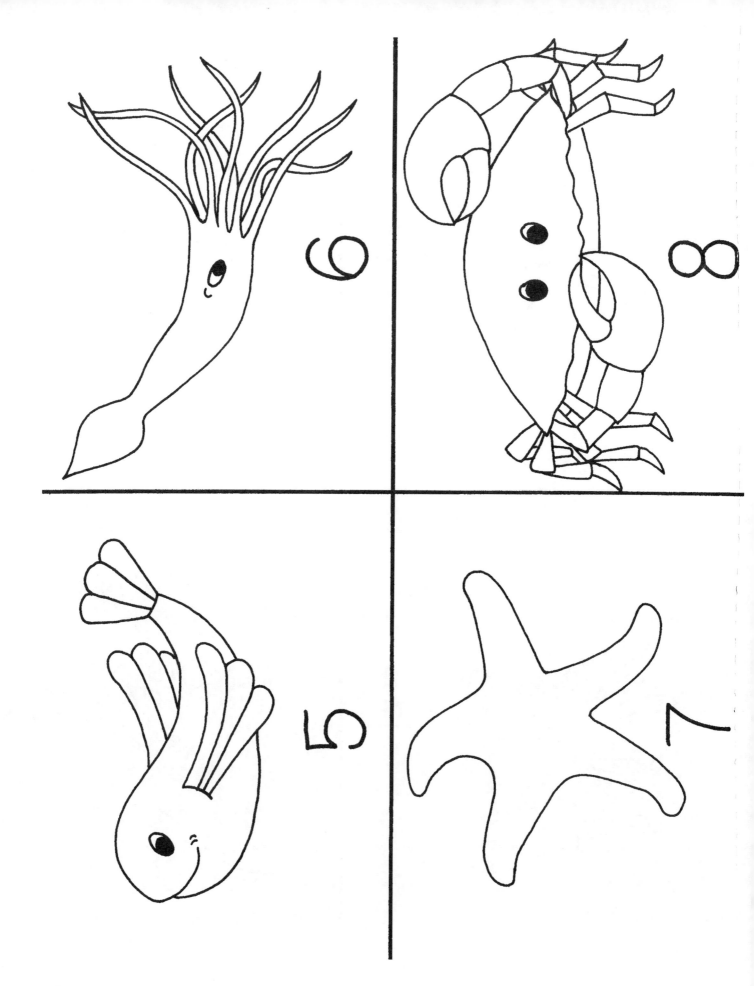

6

8

5

7

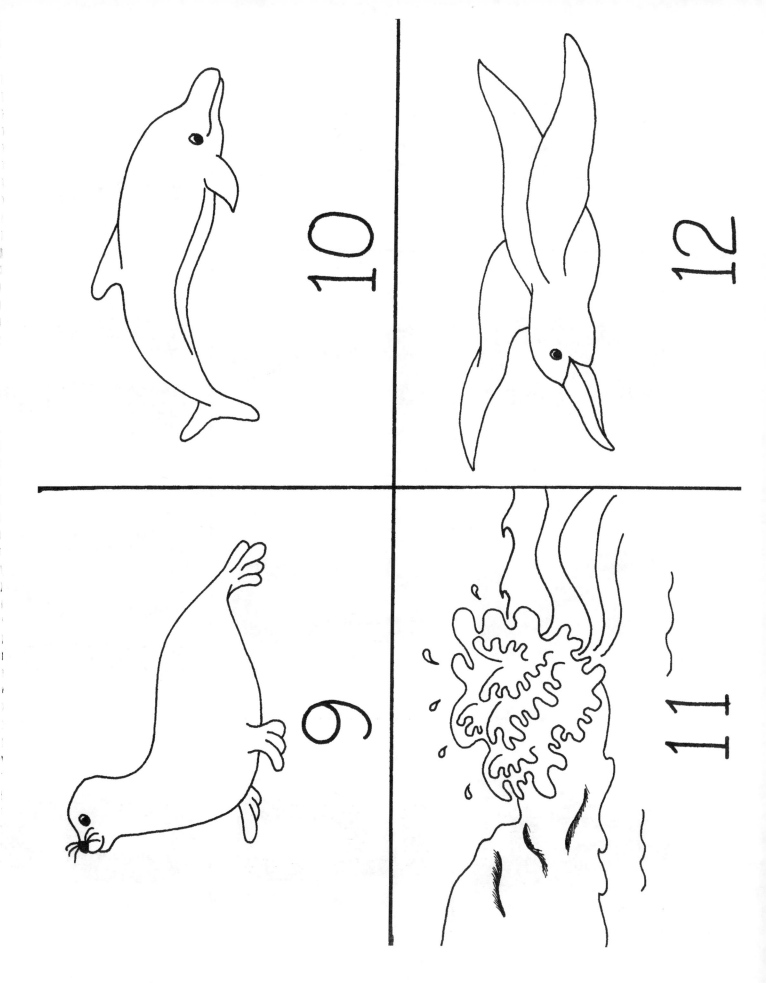

10

12

9

11

4	8	12
3	7	11
2	6	10
A	5	9

1st day	2nd day
3rd day	4th day
5th day	6th day
7th day	8th day
9th day	10th day
11th day	12th day

75